America,
Resilient Still?

———◆———

Alexander Kugushev

America, Resilient Still?

Published by Wheatmark®
2030 East Speedway Boulevard, Suite 106
Tucson, Arizona 85719 USA
www.wheatmark.com

ISBN: 978-1-62787-910-1
ISBN: 978-1-62787-911-8
LCCN: 2021922540

Bulk ordering discounts are available through Wheatmark, Inc. For more information, email orders@wheatmark.com or call 1-888-934-0888.

Contents

Premise

———◆———

Resilience energizes and drives society upward and onward. In its absence, progress stalls.

In 2007–08, I wrote *Resilient America*. In that book, I examined how Americans have responded to the succession of adverse events that have regularly marked America's history, beginning with its birth pangs in the 1790s. I noted how after each successive crisis, the American people resiliently regained societal equilibrium while verbally despairing over their country's putative decline. Lamentations continued, but all the while prosperity rose, and Americans observed their basic institutions: laws, the Constitution, the legitimacy of the political system, and a consensus on acceptable standards and behaviors. I concluded that the American character and culture had remained fundamentally consistent and resilient. (Of course, there have always been some outliers who cannot overcome human nature's worst impulses.)

Now, however, things may be different. Since the publication of *Resilient America,* four significant events have occurred, each affecting the next one:

In 2008–2011, as the logical result of manifold greed and irresponsibility, a major recession took the country by surprise.

In 2008, Americans elected a Black man to the presidency, an action unimaginable only a few short decades earlier.

In 2016, they elected another highly improbable candidate, possibly in reaction to his predecessor, with consequences as yet not fully known or understood.

In 2020, covid-19 struck. Its effects on many lives, public health, the economy, and society may linger.

Some of these events were unforeseeable and came unexpectedly; some were unprecedented. Except for covid-19, they resulted from long-term processes as time and circumstances wrought changes on our culture. They also happened while other profound developments unsettled our society. Automation and robotization alter the economy and threaten jobs and personal prospects, online commerce imperils many businesses, climate change hangs over our future, racial discord and disputes over immigration persist, and the threat of extremist violence simmers. The ambiguous effect of social media provides additional discomforts. For some, aftershocks of 9/11 still linger.

Are these accumulated stresses affecting, perhaps changing, the culture of our society? Could they have undermined, as never before, the country's ability to recover resiliently? This book sets out to examine these questions by taking a long-range cultural and historical perspective and a politically centrist position.

Chapter 1

Four Shocks

On September 14, 2008, Lehman Brothers, a major investment firm, declared bankruptcy, the largest instance in US
history at that time. The next day, stock markets plummeted,
and the Dow closed 499 points down at 10,917. These events
set into motion a succession of shocks, some coincidental
but all linked to each other. They have affected *all* Americans
in differing ways.

The United States is a great nation—not because of its
wealth, large population, or impressive armies but because
of its culture. That culture churns out incessantly new ideas
in all domains that not only keep it vital but influence the
world. People all over the globe wear jeans, eat hamburgers,
use Facebook, watch our TV shows and movies, imitate our
national parks (we invented those too), buy our stocks, trust
our dollar, and copy our politics, for better or worse. All that

is the product of a diverse, dynamic, energetic, self-confident, and optimistic people.

I ask whether that confidence and optimism have been shaken by the four specific shocks I describe below. In effect, I investigate the state of our psychic resilience as we, as Americans, live through the aftershocks and forge this nation's future.

Between 2008 and 2020, four successive shocks struck our society. The Great Recession of 2008–2011 directly affected millions when they lost their homes and jobs, but it also indirectly touched all of us as the economy teetered. The election of a Black man to the presidency stupefied, if not always consciously, countless Americans. The election of his unconventional successor dismayed millions. To these economic and political upheavals, covid-19 added fears and uncertainty for all.

The major significance of this sequence of events is that they don't stand in isolation from each other. They form a chain, as each link influenced the subsequent ones. Together, they have caused a prodigious social, cultural, political, and economic avalanche of disruptions over only twelve years.

The avalanche challenges our resilience. Shock after shock, it grew in stages. Large numbers fell victim to the major 2008–2011 recession. Many among these (and others as well) absorbed a cultural shock from the election of Barack Obama. For them, the inconceivable happened: a Black president with a Muslim-seeming name yet, a Democrat to boot (the party that favors government, and the government had failed to protect them from the recession). The Obama election deepened and radicalized some of our existing cleavages.

In this economic and political climate, the Tea Party emerged. This movement expressed the growing resentment of non-Hispanic Whites toward the erosion of their traditional cultural dominance. The cocktail of emotions included reactions to illegal immigration, the government's heavy hand, the ethnic diversification of America, the rise of Blacks into positions of prominence and equality, and the feeling of being left behind by growing economic disparities and cultural distancing.[1]

A very unhappy portion of the electorate was ready for Donald Trump in 2016. He campaigned to return the country to pre-Obama times—in fact, to a mythical past—which, of course, deeply upset and alienated the other portion of the electorate. Trump's presidency deliberately accentuated the differences. When covid-19 hit in 2020, it flourished amid conditions of uncertainty and division. Policies issuing from the federal government often contradicted those of state governors and sometimes agreed with some of them—to the detriment of the population's health.

The deep recession, the two radically contrasting presidencies, and the pandemic converged with preexisting concerns and fears. Job losses from the automation and robotization of industry, the exportation of American jobs to other countries, climate change that can affect the lives of our young, the tumultuous reckonings of our racial discord, the uncontrolled migration across our borders, and the meteoric rise of online retail with the destruction of brick-and-mortar commerce all add to the avalanche and contribute to uncertainty about our future. Enough to sap our confidence?

Here we are in the 2020s, and America the Exceptional finds itself in exceptionally turbulent circumstances. Politically, many don't speak to each other anymore. Medically, epidemics threaten our lives. Technologically, we have unleashed innovations that jeopardize the livelihoods of millions. An unending storm of unconnected news and information from unverified sources compounds uncertainty as it doesn't give us time to absorb the latest story before the next one appears.

Armageddon? Well, perhaps . . . but maybe not. We need to recover the exceptional America of our aspirations. To find our way back, we must understand how we got here. Let's consider the genesis of each shock.

2008

The Great Recession of 2008–2011 delivered a most ominous shock. It showed the failure of our national character and then spilled over into subsequent events. Skullduggery, corruption, and greed were not invented in 2008. They go back repeatedly all the way to the republic's founding days. What differed this time was the staggering scale of this betrayal of American ideals and implicit trust. Unlike the Great Depression of 1929, which resulted from exuberant misjudgments, the Great Recession struck devastatingly from deliberately dishonest and irresponsible actions. Many became complicit in this debacle: Congress, government regulators, banks and other lenders, and the borrowers themselves. The lenders brought cynical greed, cupidity, and often malfeasance; the borrowers reckless ignorance; the government loose legislation and lax regulatory supervision.

None of this gloriously depicted America the Exceptional. It began some fifteen years before the 2008 crisis unfurled. In the early 1990s, the Clinton administration wanted to expand home ownership—a laudable goal. Congress, however, passed laws in 1992 and 1994 whose effects encouraged irresponsibility.[2] These laws relaxed borrowing standards to lower down payments from the usual 20% to 5%, thus enticing those who couldn't normally afford home ownership to apply for loans. The new laws also intentionally weakened regulatory supervision of the lending industry, which had lobbied and greased to steer this legislation. Now the loans were made to the unwary on deceptive, predatory terms. Banks and other lending operations like Fannie Mae invented obscure financial instruments—mortgage-backed securities, collateralized debt obligations—to conceal nefarious manipulations of the system and enrich themselves.[3] This debacle betrayed the immigrant ethic that supports our national character (more about that in chapter 4: "Immigrants: Agents of Resilience"). Lenders and borrowers, in complicity, left nine million unemployed and some ten million foreclosed homes. At the peak of the recession, the economy stood on the brink of collapse. Although, by 2014, thanks to the new administration continuing to inject immense amounts of money, the economy had recovered, the human damage remained profound. Much harm to our

resilience ensued from this scandalous recession. It carried
pessimism over into the next three shocks. Many lost confidence in the government and in our institutions. Hostility
toward *any* immigrants, legal or illegal, increased as they were
now viewed as competitors for scarce jobs. Unemployment
in 2010 stood at 9.6%. All bad for national resilience.

In *Open, the Story of Human Progress,* Johan Norberg cites
considerable psychological research that indicates that
racism strongly increased in a climate of economic uncertainty.[4] In that climate, Barack Obama appeared.

Obama!

In America, we know that the impossible just takes a little
longer. We walked on the moon, invented the internet and,
elected a Black man as president. The last was an unimaginable act for most Americans even a decade earlier. Barack
Obama's momentous election stretches our understanding
of America, where the impossible can arrive sooner than
expected.

The path to that election began with the GI Bill of 1944.
Over more than three generations, it added a very large
college-educated cohort to our society. Education can do
wondrous things. It can open the mind to the new, to the
unknown, to the unimaginable. For many but not for all. By
2008, a large portion of the electorate was ready for Obama.

Obama had gifts—intelligence, energy, eloquence—
and he could think big. He was well educated and worldly.
When he made speeches, he spoke American. Everybody

could understand: those who approved and those many who didn't. (Full disclosure: I voted for him twice, although I am neither a Democrat or a liberal. I did it because to judge an individual by what they could do, not by the color of their skin, is, to me, American in the purest sense.)

Under Obama's presidency, America never reached the consensus of confidence and optimism that leads to national resilience. Millions who lost their jobs and homes in the Great Recession needed to put their lives together. Many other millions, upset by Obama's election, began to react to it. The country floated out of kilter despite the economy gradually stabilizing. Obama's presidency years served to persistently upset almost half the population. For many, culture overrode economics. The constant promotion of diversity in its many forms by Obama's liberals raised much hostility, especially among non-Hispanic Whites. In chapter 2, I stress that for full societal resilience to blossom, a consensus must form around the *center* of public opinion. The opposite happened under Obama. Opinions receded from the center.

The intensity of the Obama shock to a certain idea of America caused latent cultural tensions to coalesce into the unexpected Tea Party. It spoke for those White Americans who felt themselves slipping to the margins of a society that increasingly accepted the unprecedented. Metropolitan elites scorned them for their views on race, religion, guns, and immigrants. Economic forces shipped their jobs by the millions to China. The attack on their traditional culture sharpened with the election of a Black man to the presidency. The Tea Party swept the 2010 congressional election.

On that Black man now concentrated the accumulated
resentments and ire. Poisonous conspiracy theories aimed
to brand him as illegitimate. His most ferocious opponents
promoted the notion that he was a secret Muslim, born in
Kenya. You know, Kenya—where those Black guys are.
Donald Trump led that chorus. In speaking with those who
disapproved of Obama, I heard that he was a socialist, that
he had no experience with business, that he was this, that
he was that. All denied fervently that they opposed him on
racial grounds. A CBS poll, however, reported in 2010 that
30% of Tea Party members were birthers and that another
25% claimed they didn't know where Obama was born.
Which suggests that fewer than half of Tea Partiers didn't
oppose him on racial grounds.[5] The 2009 bailouts of lenders
helped big banks and companies but still left millions unemployed. This stoked populist resentment of government and
paved the road for the election of Donald Trump.

Obama's presidency didn't help our resilience. It exac-
erbated partisan hostility and removed the prospect of
respectful discourse among Americans. The center, where
resilience dwells, faded.

Trump!

Trump's election bared the distance between two parallel
Americas. Both believe in the country's fundamentals: the
virtue of our Constitution, the equality of all before the law,
fairness to others, and the other convictions that should
unite us (which I review in the chapter 3 section "What unites

us"). However, Trump's campaign and election revealed the extent to which these two Americas differ in how they interpret fundamentals, such as the meaning of the Constitution or equality of all before the law. They live in diverging cultures, a crucial issue for our resilience, which requires consensus (and which I explore in chapter 9, "The March of Our Culture").

Of the two Americas, one (let's call it metropolitan) accepts and promotes change. The other (let's call it populist) tends to shy away from change, suspicious of it. The former predominates in big cities, the latter in smaller communities and tends to express conservative and nativist feelings. The metropolitans live in a swirl of generally better-educated, multiethnic, multicultural groups in constant transition. The populists live largely in enduring, mostly White, English-only-speaking communities in which happenings in places like New York or San Francisco may appear culturally alien.

Generalizing broadly, one of these Americas elected Obama, the other Trump. As I traced the election of Obama to the GI Bill of 1944, let's also examine the roots of the Tea Party and of the sentiments that led to Trump's election. At the very origin of the republic, the two Americas already coexisted. One (comprised of Boston, New York, Philadelphia, and even Charleston) faced the Atlantic with its international connections. The other looked west, to the interior of the continent, as it expanded the frontier.

We can follow the split between the two Americas over some three hundred years. Already in the eighteenth century, waves of Scots-Irish arrived into colonial Pennsylvania. The English from metropolitan Philadelphia kept pushing them farther and farther west until they eventually settled in then-remote Appalachia. Their descendants and others continued into Kentucky, Ohio, and Tennessee, broadening the frontier, moving culturally away from the Atlantic cities. With the election of Andrew Jackson and the defeat of John Quincy Adams in 1828, the two Americas confronted each other. The Civil War provided the next episode as the more rural South lost to the industrialized, immigrant-receptive North. Over a career of more than thirty years around the turn of the twentieth century, William Jennings Bryan staged an oratorical populist battle with metropolitan America. During the Great Depression, Okies arrived in California to find an alien metropolitan society.[6] Bryan's and Okies' descendants voted in 1964 for Senator Barry Goldwater, the voice of the right wing of the Republican Party.

Their day arrived with the Tea Party and Donald Trump. Unfortunately, they found America divided through no fault of their own. Since Goldwater days, metropolitan America has accelerated changes vertiginously. It does so across social, cultural, and economic domains, establishing scientific and technological inventions and innovations, separating itself ever more from a conservative, more traditional America. At the same time, reverse migrations began and continue to this day. Individuals of a more conservative disposition began abandoning Los Angeles and ultra-liberal San Francisco for Salt Lake City, Tucson, and Texas. Similarly, they left Chicago and New York for the more welcoming traditionalist South. Conversely, the liberally inclined migrated from conservative communities to a metropolitan life. The country segregated into blue and red. Trump understood all that.

The nation's history of frontiers, immigration, and constant, vigorous change created a culture that required a centrist compromise. For 240 years, the two Americas lived together and by and large maintained a social, cultural, and political dialogue. Both sides voted, played baseball, partook of popular culture, went to church, found comfort in communities, and progressed economically (the Civil War, of course, excepted). But since 1945, distances in culture, education, and economic prospects grew.

In that changed atmosphere, a Black president was perhaps a step too far for nativist sentiment, which found its voice in Trump. Trump's administration pleased many Americans but outraged others. That division caused prospects for resilience to recede further. The distances, incomprehension, and suspicions between the two Americas grew. Optimism and mutual trust shrank. The surprise of Trump's election baffled the metropolitans because they no longer had a connection or dialogue with populists. In the Obama/Trump rift, we have retreated from the traditional tolerant and consensual American center. Since, throughout his presidency, Trump catered only to his populist base, dialogue across the divide never took place.

The November 2020 election brought clarity about the cultural separation between the two sides. The 74 million who voted for Trump did it for various reasons. Some because they approved of his policies; some because he opposed immigration, illegal and legal; some because he sent subtle and unsubtle racist messages; some in general protest against cultural diversity changes; some for fear of socialism; some well-to-do because he increased their wealth; some because Trump's abrasive persona stood for them confronting a changing world they mistrusted. The 81 million who voted for his opponent did it for mainly one reason: their loathing of Trump. These included independents and disaffected Republicans, uninterested otherwise in a Democratic program. That program nevertheless motivated millions. It included the full ideological menu opposed by Trump supporters: science-based issues like public health, environment preservation, and global warming; social concerns about race and ethnicity, diversity, and income distribution; and the role of government. For that part of America, the mob attack on Congress of January 6, 2021, symbolized the conclusion of the Trump presidency.

Thus, in the wake of the 2020 election, the two Americas remained facing each other with their respective agendas clearly delineated. For the good of the country, we must recognize the legitimacy of the concerns of both sides. We, meaning all of us, need to close the gap and seek considered dialogue to revive resilience. It is our national priority. Neither side holds a monopoly on virtue, no matter what it believes.

Covid-19

Covid-19 struck unannounced and found us unprepared. At this writing, the ultimate consequences of this epidemic remain unknown. We may tame it, or it may mutate and reappear in a new and dangerous form. Nor do we know its ultimate effect on our resilience. For many Americans, it has brought fear, dented confidence, and shaken optimism. Googling discovers multiple research reports in the first twelve months of the pandemic about its psychological consequences. The research reveals that up to 40% of Americans experienced depression, fear, anxiety, and loneliness. For many, the mental health toll included abusing opioids and contemplating or even committing suicide.

Politically and socially, covid-19 has separated us further into mask-wearers and vaccine-cravers and anti-maskers and antivaxxers. Belief in science stands as the dividing line and echoes our politics. Covid-19 has brought to the surface doubts about science harbored by millions of Americans. Some political leaders disputed and disdained the advice of scientists. Private citizens displayed a suspicion of vaccines. The pandemic also brought into question the role and performance of government, split into federal, state, and local dissonant responses. In some instances, state governments did well and not so well in others. As a political polarizer, covid-19 distanced us from the center.

Covid-19 has also brought to the surface public health vulnerabilities that we ignored. It derailed the economy, creating millions of unemployed and destroying businesses large and small. Its shock to our society has also accelerated processes already underway, principally the effects of ever-increasing automation of work and sparking online activities such as shopping or meetings. Suddenly, overnight, entire categories of occupations became unneeded, while a rapid creation of new businesses faces uncertainty (more on that in chapter 7: "The Economy in Novel Times").

Disastrously, covid-19 has disrupted education. Since

concern about our resilience explicitly involves our future, the most harmful consequence of this epidemic will befall education. Our absolute priority requires that we correct without delay and through creative solutions the immeasurable consequences of our young not having attended school. From personal experience, I can testify to how damaging absence from school can be. In turmoil during the Second World War, I lost an academic year as an early teenager. I never fully recovered. Children and adolescents need uninterrupted, incremental learning. That eluded me as the war tossed me hither and yon. In chapter 8 (in the section "Policies"), I make a specific proposal to address our pressing education problems.

Furthermore, covid-19 has inflicted monumental harm on the world's economy. In this sense, the twelve-year sequence of four shocks comes full circle. It began with an economic catastrophe and concludes with another. Paradoxically, however, covid-19 has accelerated the modernization of the delivery of health service from too much paper and unnecessary face-to-face interaction to digitalization and efficient online encounters. This conversion will launch a major industry. Venture capitalists are licking their chops. I address the consequences of covid-19 in more detail in subsequent chapters.

Overall, then, covid-19 has caused great harm to health and to the economy. But you can't keep a good nation down. After initial disarray—unemployment in April 2020 at 14.8%, a sharp stock market plunge, and businesses closing, some forever—the institutions and the people began to respond. The Federal Reserve quickly stabilized the dollar, providing confidence for the world economy.[7] Stocks rebounded, and unemployment dropped to 7.8% in September and 6.2% in February 2021. In its very first year, the pandemic began to create new businesses, certainly in the pharmaceutical industry but many simply as an unstoppable extension of the American entrepreneurial spirit. The US Census Bureau reported that new business applications soared in 2020 to some 550,000 (they had reached a high mark of near 300,000 in 2019). Resilience sprouting, defying disaster.

As we struggle to absorb forces and counterforces produced by the four successive shocks, we simultaneously experience other powerful concerns. The changing climate reminds us of potential danger. Nor can we ignore the effects, positive and negative, of social media. Automation and online commerce continue to grow explosively with not fully foreseeable consequences—bad for some, good for others— along with disruption for many and profound changes in our behaviors. Millions of jobs lost, some temporarily, very many definitely. Amid these psychological and practical stresses, racial confrontations remain an issue in American history that we have never settled.

So here we stand, cleft in two or more societally and politically, wounded economically, culturally uncertain, facing our future. Is it all dismal, or will our character reassert itself as in the past? That is the question: how is our psychic resilience doing amid all the turbulence? Some of the above speaks of confusion, but the aftermath of covid-19 hints at a spirited recovery, at least of business.[8] Energetic entrepreneurs exhibit outsized resilience. They make the gross domestic product grow but for whom? For all?

> ***Why resilience matters.*** Throughout this book, I return to the theme of resilience. Why does it matter? Resilience is an individual characteristic but expresses itself in a social context. Our disunited society, as it is in the early 2020s, doesn't foster resilience. A large portion of our people pines for an imagined past. Another large portion pushes for an imagined future. They move culturally in opposite directions, but resilience requires consensus. Externally, too, the absence of resilience imperils us. Countries that don't wish us well—China, Russia, and others—have studied us carefully and understand/act on our vulnerabilities, of which our divisions are the main ones. For reasons internal and external, we need to regain our normal resilience.

Let's look next at how American resilience operates.

Chapter 2

American Resilience

Americans always end up doing the right thing,
after having tried everything else.

—Winston Churchill, who had an American mother

Some doubt that Churchill said that, but some of us like
to believe it because it expresses so well the mechanism of
American resilience. Indeed, among Americans' outstanding
character traits, psychic resilience stands out. After every
adversity, it has pulled the country back in short order onto
its positive, ever-upward march. Can it now—in the wake of
those four shocks?

★ ★ ★

I am an immigrant, invested spiritually and by conviction in America and concerned about the prospects of my valued investment.

Immigrants tend to bring high, idealistic expectations of America. Fareed Zakaria, an immigrant (from India) and a distinguished intellect, in his book *Ten Lessons for a Post-Pandemic Word,* concludes that the American people have lost their way over recent decades. He gives examples from governance, business, competition with China, unreadiness for the digital world, and more. His opinions would lead us to question the resilience of present-day Americans because his observations point to an apparently stagnating country.

An immigrant from many parts, I have come to a different conclusion—that going astray is a normal condition in America's evolution. Our history provides numerous examples. My life in the United States has led me to believe that Winston Churchill's above quotation captures the essence of the American character: restless, enterprising, change-creating, past-destroying, risk-seeking, given to excess, but able to correct errors. Therefore, prone to recover resiliently. Hence, I don't believe that Zakaria's skepticism takes the American character into account. Though, this time, who knows? Too early to tell.

Going astray

The American people have gone astray repeatedly. It's a tradition. Already in the 1790s, political factions went at each other's throats, risking tearing the young union apart and spurred by an out-of-control press (even then!). The 1820s brought new convulsions as the populist frontier wrested power from the Federalist establishment, while the South began to confront the North. The 1840s and '50s saw rising conflicts between slavery and abolition, culminating in a civil war. The last three decades of the nineteenth century boiled in massive corruption, uncontrolled skullduggery in business, collapse of crop prices in agricultural states, labor strife, and lawlessness in the West. In the 1920s, Prohibition and the KKK combined to produce much violence and crime as that decade crashed into the Great Depression. In the wake of John Kennedy's assassination, the country fell into cultural and economic chaos in the 1960s and '70s. Beginning in 2008, we have absorbed successive economic, political, and public health shocks. Seems it's the American way.

Where does the American character stand today? What destiny are we forging? Is the United States still on its habitual path of resilience, the compass needle still pointing firmly north, or can we detect an inflection point like those that signaled the decline of other imperial powers or other successful civilizations? Is today's America like Athens in the fifth century BC, riven by internal rivalries and an epidemic, creating its own demise? Or like Rome in the second century AD, having lost its republican discipline, when it began to lose its direction? Or does seventeenth-century England provide a better metaphor in its confrontation between an autocratic king and a constitutional parliament? That produced a civil war, but the nation survived and went on to greatness—a perhaps particularly pertinent example since we have inherited England's culture.

How our resilience operates

History has presented the American people with frequent crises, mostly economic but also social and political. Every one became a test of their resilience. From each, with no exception, they have bounced back, generally in short order. Their society's inexhaustible energy and instinctive confidence pulled them through. Appendix 1 presents the data on the frequency and length of each economic crisis.

Every critical juncture required the full display of the components of Americans' resilience: a positive disposition with an openness to change, a suppleness and adaptability of character, and the toughness and capacity to recover quickly from difficulties. These qualities have served Americans well for over 240 years and even before.

> We need to retain those two indispensable
> conditions that trigger American resilience:
> confidence and optimism. In their absence,
> resilience remains dormant.

One additional condition must exist. Our resilience needs to emanate from the social and political center; it fails to arise from the polarized extremes. The center forms when a majority of Americans can agree on fundamental values and establish a consensual dialogue. Which is why we have only two meaningful political parties, both centrist, despite oratorical fireworks that can mislead one to think otherwise.

Recovery

Our society drifted uncertainly during the socially, politically, and economically chaotic 1960s and '70s. But in the
mid-1980s, America had regained its resilient self. People
started families again, even getting married; professors
graded students rigorously; inventors invented profusely; the
stock market went up; inflation and unemployment down;
the Republican president (Reagan) maintained an adversarial but genial relationship with the Democratic speaker
of the house (O'Neil). I discuss this transformation further
below, but let's remain on how full that recovery became.

Resilience amid economic turbulence

The economy constantly tests our resilience. Financial
crises have visited us often and regularly. There resides in
the American character an exceeding, at times reckless,
instinct for risk-taking in pursuit of material gain. Indeed,
Americans carry to an excess the cultural gene of ambition
to become wealthy. Far from all Americans, of course, equate
success with acquisition of money. But enough do to foment
economic crises. As a consequence, the United States goes
through periodic financial downturns that undermine the
optimism and confidence requisite to trigger resilience.

Facing down crises

Financial crises began already in the late 1790s and have
never abated. Especially telling were the recoveries from the
panics and the depression of the 1890s and from the Great

Depression of the 1930s. By the late nineteenth century, the country suffered repeated economic calamities caused by widespread speculation and malfeasance. A depression from 1882 to 1887, which included a panic in 1884, preceded a series of economic shocks in the 1890s. The effects of another panic in 1893 extended for several years. It entailed runs on banks with massive bank closures, bankruptcies in some industries, and explosive anger in agricultural states in the Midwest and the South over tumbling prices of farm products. A far-left Populist Party arose in response and had temporary success. The country appeared in disarray, with no visible direction or leadership. But within a decade, responding to Teddy Roosevelt's sunny energy and optimism ("Believe you can and you're halfway there"), the United States had returned to its natural can-do, risk-accepting self, reflecting its cultural resilience.

That recovery was not a mere act of Teddy Roosevelt's magic. He provided confidence and optimism at the right time. Much of the recovery actually grew gradually from outrage-driven Americans. Workers went on strike, sometimes bloodily. Muckrakers raked the abundant muck in business and government. In *The Jungle,* Upton Sinclair[1] exposed a range of social ills, including the ruthless lack of hygiene in Chicago's slaughter houses. Jane Addams drove social reform. Much progressive legislation became enacted, establishing the rights of workers. The new laws checked the malefactors of great wealth and broke up the monopolies. At the turn of the twentieth century, the country was regaining its balance as Teddy Roosevelt providentially inherited the presidency. His persona provided the latent boost. He speechified vigorously, passed confidence-building laws, sent the Great White Fleet around the world, and started building the Panama Canal on stolen land. The now-optimistic country entered the new century as a power to be reckoned with. A story about the operation of American resilience. (Of course, then it was a White Anglo-Saxon America since, unlike now, people of any other color or ethnicity didn't count. Now, much more diverse, do we retain those cultural mechanisms that can allow us to bounce back like then? I believe that at its core the American Spirit is immune to race, religion, and ethnicity. Hence our increasing diversity will not prevent our cultural mechanisms to continue to function.)

Resilience deserves a special look during the Great Depression of the 1930s. For very large numbers of Americans, dire social and economic conditions dominated that decade. We remember it as a time of misery and retreat from American buoyancy, so dramatically portrayed in John Steinbeck's *The Grapes of Wrath*.[2] This view is only partly true. During those years, much of society continued to function, though at a reduced pace and in an emergency mood. The federal government stepped in with energetic investment to provide employment and maintain the foundations of normality. Much was built, materially and spiritually. The Empire State Building went up, Pan Am crossed the Pacific, the colossal Boulder (now Hoover) Dam was built. So were countless schools, police and fire stations, government buildings, libraries, courthouses, and airports. Gutzon Borglum carved the presidents in the great, now politically controversial, monument on Mount Rushmore. The government

provided support for the arts, and they thrived. The national
parks received maintenance and enhancement. Hollywood
filmed streams of light entertainment. And Seabiscuit caught
the imagination of the depressed.

The misery lasted a full decade. In 1938, unemployment still stood at 19%. Despite that, sparks of resilience
flew. Not few among those who worked on government-
sponsored projects, the Works Progress Administration particularly, attested to commitment to and pride in the results
of their work. Studs Terkel recounts such anecdotes in *Hard
Times*.[3] So does James McGovern in *A Time for Hope: Americans
in the Great Depression*.[4] He wrote how many Americans faced
the Depression years with resilience, optimism, confidence,
abundant energy, and robust action; how, with the New Deal's
help, social and cultural resources stabilized society and
fostered the resilience with which it withstood its severe trials.

We need to again ascribe such manifestations of resilience to confidence spurred by leadership from above. FDR
strove to maintain the people's spirit intact. At his inaugura-
tion, he proclaimed, "We have nothing to fear but fear itself"
and continued to project a jaunty and confident attitude
throughout the 1930s. The people reelected him repeatedly
because he stimulated their spiritual resilience.

Culture and resilience

Political and social crises also measure our national
resilience. As in economic ones, this resilience depends
intimately on optimism. The Civil War tested our institutions to the core. The victorious North quickly emerged
fully resilient, confident, and buoyed by optimism. It built

railroads at breakneck speed, and its population rapidly spread westward. It expanded education across the land by creating many new colleges and universities, mainly agricultural. It also unleashed an orgy of corruption, the other facet of human nature. Resilience does not equate to virtue. The defeated South sank into a prolonged stagnation, economically and spiritually, as it had no cause for optimism.

World War II, an undoubted crisis, also tested our wills and our institutions. Again, the victorious country came roaring back in short order. There was much to be optimistic about. In 1945, the United States emerged as incomparably the globally richest and militarily most powerful country.

The aftermaths of the Civil War and World War II demonstrated the interdependence between optimism and confidence. In both instances, the victors had also retained confidence in their basic institutions: in the law, the constitutional system of governance, community spirit, religion, and the assumptions and standards of a shared culture. As that basis remained stable for a majority of Americans, it fostered optimism. But when doubt penetrates our civic confidence, optimism wanes.

The assassination of John Kennedy in 1963 shook the nation's confidence. The troubling circumstances of the crime and the uncertain and suspect investigation that followed left an agitated public. Having only recently immigrated, I remember vividly how, over the next few months and then over the following decade, the country's mood changed. Doubts arose; confidence faded. Resentments and grievances that had resided in deeper layers erupted in unfamiliar movements, in riots, and in violence. All of it was compounded by the draft into the Vietnam War. During those years, no voice from the top would sound a reassuring, confidence-restoring message. Both Johnson and Nixon struggled to justify the confidence-destroying war.

By the mid-1970s, the nation had reached a bottom of discouragement, demoralization, disorientation, and loss of faith. It sagged under the unprecedented: the Vietnam War lost; the president resigning in disgrace; all authority—civil, religious, and educational—questioned; traditional morality in disarray ("if it feels good, do it"); sex, drugs, and rock and roll everywhere; markets down; inflation up; uncertain, hirsute men reeling under the impact of feminism. Americans meandered spiritually and psychologically.[5] But observing their behaviors ten years later, one wouldn't recognize the same people. It turned out that resilience remained, but confidence needed a stimulus to resurface. At the needed moment, a confident leader's voice sounded. Ronald Reagan's sunny disposition ("It's morning in America") resonated for a majority and brought back habitual behaviors put to sleep by the turbulent decade and a half (in contrast to well-meaning Jimmy Carter's character, unsuited to the demands of presidential leadership).

Throughout difficult times, a deep reserve of resilience rested in the great majority of Americans, who continued to lead perhaps lessened but normal lives. In the economically panicky 1890s, much of America continued to function. Industry—iron, steel, railroads, agricultural machinery, even automobiles—boomed. German breweries in Milwaukee and St. Louis prospered. Immigration reached unprecedented levels. Social and cultural life grew vigorously. The

World Columbian Exhibition in Chicago in 1893 drew over 27 million visitors. The great Czech composer Antonin Dvořak spent three years in the United States (1892–1985) at the invitation of the National Conservatory of Music of America to become its director. While here, Dvořak wrote the *New World Symphony*, a milestone in the validation of American cultural significance. Though much attenuated for many, normal life continued for most Americans during the Great Depression, stoking reserves of resiliency for a happier day.

Failing and starting again illustrates another aspect of resilience. Americans are nothing if not enthusiastic, risk-taking entrepreneurs. They start hundreds of thousands of businesses yearly. In chapter 7, "The Economy in Novel Times," I discuss specifics. About half fail in their first attempt.[6] Yet year after year, about 50% or more of those who failed start again. Among those very many who tried and tried again and eventually succeeded we find Milton Hershey (Hershey's Chocolate), who endured three failures before success. Jeff Bezos, of Amazon.com, suffered a failure before trying again. Henry Ford had founded two car companies, and both failed before he succeeded with the Ford Motor Company. Walt Disney, too, failed in his first venture. All, undoubtedly, harbored deep reserves of American optimism but also confidence in the stability of their nation's institutions.

Inequality and "classes"

Inequality is inherent to the human condition. At the individual level, it derives from differences in personal ability, motivation, education, circumstances, and choices. Some enter life heavily disadvantaged by poverty and social circumstances; others start on third base. Throughout our history, inequality has naturally persisted at the individual level and, of greater concern, at a group level. More often, it negatively affected those with darker skin. For most Whites, inequality had moderate consequences because mobility and opportunity seemed limitless. Over the past half century, sharp economic inequality has become entrenched, limiting upward mobility for some. Our egalitarian society cannot accept this because persistent inequality can tear at our national unity. This, of course, doesn't favor resilience. Significantly improved education and enlightened public policy can greatly shrink the gaps. I address these themes consistently in subsequent chapters and specifically in chapter 8 (in the section on policy).

Meanwhile, we don't need to stoke additional divisions. Much debilitating talk in recent years affirms that America is divided into classes that have created entrenched economic inequality. Legitimizing such opinions questions American social dynamism. Implicitly, these views decree that our vitality has vanished and that our society has stagnated. My experience of a positive and dynamic America does not accept such views. I see a glass half full, in which cultural resilience has encouraged social mobility over three centuries.

Let's be clear: there are no classes in America. Classes are static, rigid social structures that endure over generations. They divide a society into unchangeable economic and social layers. We have instead multiple economic strata in constant motion. They allow citizens to move up and down the scale. When individuals get stuck in a particular economic stratum, we can pass laws to revitalize the mobility of that group. Viewed that way, this stratification has no adverse effect on resilience. As for talk of class inequality in America today, that implies structural injustice. Present economic inequality is, however, caused primarily by educational differences, as I discuss in chapter 5 on education.

Belief in classes leads us to beliefs that divide us. Thus, the illogical notion of the 1 percent, presumably malevolent and changeless, and the 99 percent, presumably victimized.

The membership of 1 percenters is in constant flux. The *Forbes* magazine yearly lists of wealthiest Americans describes well the reality of American life.[7] When compared over a span of twenty-five years, the membership on these lists will have completely altered. New names will have cropped up; old ones disappeared. There are no economic dynasties. Nor are there dynastic political classes. The Bushes are a fading flicker. Otherwise, new men and women dominate the political scene (and they didn't all go to Harvard). Thus, talk of technocrats and plutocrats constituting a new class of wealth and power. Consider Elon Musk. An immigrant, he built PayPal, Tesla, and SpaceX. Is he now a member of a plutocratic class, or is his a typical American story of initiative, energy, hard work, and, yes, perhaps a touch of ruthlessness?

The 99 percenters do not fit into any single category. They include wealthy businesspeople, affluent professionals, the young at the beginning of their careers, tradespeople like plumbers and electricians, unionized government employees, and, certainly, the poor. Are they all victimized by a 1 percent upper class?

Nor are the "poor" a social class. Their membership is also in constant flux. The Black American population is commonly accepted as most disadvantaged and classified as a permanent "class." Those assumptions fly in the face of our dynamic society. Particularly illuminating is an examination of the distribution of incomes among the US Black population. *Black Demographics* (August 12, 2020) reports the following about Black households:[8]

Household Income	Percent
$200,000+	3%
$150,000–$200,000	4%
$50,000–$150,000	36%
$25,000–$50,000	25%
$15,000–$25,000	13%
Less than $15,000	19%

We also had some 380,000 Black American millionaires[9] and 7 billionaires.[10] For perspective, in 1963, the poverty rate among American Blacks stood at 42%; in 2019, at 23.8%,[11] which buttresses the trend reflected in the above table (the 23.8% stems from data in the bottom two rungs of the above table). These numbers lose power, of course, when compared with household incomes of other groups. In 2019, Asian Americans have a median household income of $98,7844, Whites of $76,957, Hispanics of $56,113, and Blacks of $46,573.[12] These disparities have a detrimental effect on our common resilience, and I address them in other parts of this book. Here, I place the emphasis on the 43% of Black Americans who in 2019 fit economically into the medium to upper strata of our society. These are probably the better-educated and hence upwardly mobile and thus negate a class theory. These data also tell us that their poverty does not relegate all Black Americans to a permanent class. So are there classes in America?

> For the role of class and equality in America, I refer to my English friend Ken, born in London in a poor and little-educated family. This endowed him with a strong Cockney accent, which foreclosed doors for advancement in British, then very class-conscious society. Ken is ambitious and energetic, and he immigrated to the United States. In California, he received an education, learned computer programming, excelled at it, started his own company, and retired a success. Instant "upper class"?

Sources of our optimism and confidence

As I restate throughout my narrative, optimism is the fundamental expression of our resilience. Americans regularly utter pessimistic talk about the condition of their country and its prospects, but optimism shines through in

their behaviors and actions. I cannot emphasize strongly
enough that my experience of six decades in America has
taught me to ignore the deprecating talk and instead observe
the natives' constructive doings stemming from instinctive
American can-doism. Their collective temperament has
become by now, I speculate, part of their cultural genes
transmitted over generations.

A few months after immigrating to the United States, I
had a job teaching French and Spanish at a small Catholic
college in Pennsylvania. I shared an office with a young
history professor, a Midwesterner. He turned out to be quite
liberal, but this meant nothing to me then. I simply assumed
that a nation so successful couldn't produce anything but
sound thinkers. We got along quite well, but in a conversation, he astonished me by informing me that I had made a
big mistake in immigrating because, in this country, no hope
existed, injustice prevailed, the rich oppressed the poor, and
the American Dream had died.

I listened, but my brief experiences in this country told
me otherwise. I saw people designated as poor, but they
drove cars and had TVs. As for the American Dream dying,
my classes were full of first-college-generation sons of
semiliterate coal miners and steelworkers. Blacks, of course,
were heavily discriminated against in 1960, but I had no
experience of their lives or those of Amerindians. Little did
anyone imagine then that a Black man would become president of the United States in my lifetime. (I often wondered,
over the years, what became of my dyspeptic office mate in
this positive nation. As he matured, could he have recovered
confidence in our institutions?)

Subsequently, and often over the years, I kept hearing from the right and the left alike about the decline of America's freedom, morality, standards, prospects, and access to justice and opportunity. Liberals supported the views of my history professor informant. Conservatives provided a counterpoint. Liberals assailed the lack of change in American society, conservatives its uncontrollable acceleration. I continue to listen in some disbelief. As an immigrant, I see a quite different United States that has an optimistic spring in its step. That optimism may or may not be conscious individually, but collectively it resides in the national culture. In this book, however, I ask how bouncy that spring in the native step remains now.

American optimism is an amalgam of two essential conditions: the immigrant experience combined with the ease of becoming successful in a climate of liberty that builds self-reliance. The great majority of Americans descend from immigrants. Only optimists, possessed of a degree of self-confidence, emigrate. How easy, they found on settling, to become successful in the new continent after leaving the old world with its social and economic constraints. In America, immigrants found infinite spaces, rich soils, vast forests, bountiful rivers and sea coasts, where land was cheap or free (provided, perhaps, that one killed some Indigenous Americans). But most importantly, they found open attitudes and egalitarian behaviors. They encountered no social barriers, no classes. One forged a new identity, with maybe a new name, and found that the laws protected one's freedom to act and to move. None of this, of course, reflected the experiences of nonimmigrant Blacks or Amerindians.

Resilience in our lore

Everyday language reveals deeply felt convictions. Let's consider how it reveals optimism. How rarely do we hear the term *resignation* in American discourse and how much more frequently *expectation* or *aspiration*? Like *resignation*, the word *difficulty* became banned from everyday American speech, replaced by *challenge*. *Difficulty* connotes an obstacle hard to overcome. *Challenge*, instead, implies a positive attitude: attacking an obstacle with an expectation of success. The frontier experience has spawned other American character traits that buttress our optimism: an independence of spirit, onward and upward mobility, and initiative in seeking and seizing opportunity. These traits engendered self-reliance because circumstances placed the decision-making burden on the individual. An irrepressible, all-encompassing drive to promote improvement, and hence, change followed.

Add another implicitly optimistic trait: an almost genetic drive for problem-solving and inventiveness. Pessimists will not spend their evenings inventing because their temperament doesn't anticipate favorable outcomes. But optimistic Americans have produced cascades of inventions year after year since colonial days. Some famed inventors like Benjamin Franklin, Samuel Morse, Thomas Edison, Alexander Graham Bell, and Nikola Tesla are part of the pantheon. Let's consider a random sample of inventions among many thousands: the assembly line, the cotton gin, the typewriter, the zipper, the hearing aid, dental floss, the pacemaker, the artificial heart, the photograph, traffic lights, radiocarbon dating, antilock brakes, the personal computer, and a crowning jewel—the internet and all the inventions it continues to generate. Ah,

but do we still invent? I turn to that in chapter 6 on invention
and innovation.

Resilience wobbles

The culture of this immigrant nation has, over time, accumulated a capital of optimistic beliefs and behaviors leading
to resilient outcomes and personal success. But it has also
led to less desirable results. Optimism thrives in an environment where everything facilitates success if one has a dose
of initiative and courage. Unbounded optimism carries risks,
however, as our multiple economic recessions have shown.
Those possessed of the optimistic gene may also falter
morally. When that gene runs amok, it produces market
crashes. By 2008, many Americans and their bankers had
forgotten that irresponsibility has consequences. A torrent
of unsupported real estate loans crushed the economy. It is
not clear at this point whether lessons have been learned
and translated into more responsible behaviors conducive
to resilience. Answering that question is part of this book's
central aim.

Optimistic resilience can fail among considerable
segments of American society, especially during testing
times. The *Washington Post* (May 27, 2020) informs us, "A
third of Americans are showing signs of clinical anxiety or
depression, Census Bureau data shows, the most definitive
and alarming sign yet of the psychological toll exacted by the
coronavirus pandemic." Who belongs to this huge portion of
our population so at odds with the usually smiley disposition
of the American public? Further, scattered studies suggest
that most of that depressed population is over sixty-five

years old. Should we deduce that two-thirds of us, mostly younger, remain immune to the psychological toll?

Recent years have brought a succession of economic, cultural, and public health shocks that may have affected our ability to recover. Plentiful crime and violence and acerbic race relationships run against the positive American grain. Certainly, many Blacks and Amerindians have little reason and scarce confidence to feel as full members of our society.

Will we buckle? Will we elastically bounce back? To answer these questions, and as we progress through this book, we must investigate the presence or absence of confidence and optimism. In the following chapters, I explore whether my hope, optimism, and confidence in a better future remain justified under the current historical circumstances.

Let's start with an exploration of emotions and behaviors that stand in our way and beliefs that may help us reassert our resilience.

Chapter 3

Separations and Convergence

---◆---

In this chapter, I examine what separates us and what should unite us. Our separations stem from current emotions—a product of too-rapid economic, social, and cultural change—but also from societal discords of long duration, such as race, religion, and gun violence. Separations, it turns out, operate at the collective level. What can unite us lies in a profounder, individual, instinctive, and enduring layer of our national character. Our resilience suffers from the separations but benefits when we unite.

What divides us

Some of our divisions have existed for decades, if not for centuries. Others have come to a simmer more recently. Yet others boil as a result of the four shocks described in chapter 1. Ever-accelerating cultural, scientific, and technological changes, on top of the four shocks, have sharpened our disunions. The media has deliberately intensified them. Dedicated television channels financially thrive from our divisions, which they promote. Social media provides a megaphone to expand this distancing. Hence, the more vitriolic politics. Hence, an encompassing atmosphere of crisis. Each of the following oppositions detracts from a national consensus, from optimism and confidence.

Education
STATUS: **SIMMERING**

Growing disparities in education today cause our most consequential divergences. Those who read and those who don't access different sources of information. The former read *The Economist* to learn about world affairs; the others read magazines to learn about affairs in Hollywood. In a civic sense, this may not matter—we all have the right to our personal choices. But in a practical sense, it affects our individual destinies. We live in a knowledge- and science-based modern world, and levels of education affect it all: our economy, our politics, our employment, our ability to innovate, and our personal place in society. Over the next decade, millions of Americans will lose their jobs because of automation and robotization. The majority will be the less educated. Conversely, the better educated will prosper from participation in technological and scientific advances.

Most American parents want their children to receive an education. What that means differs. For some, a high school with a successful football team and modest academics proves satisfactory. For others, a school satisfies parents when it prepares their children for an academic scholarship to a leading university. The better educated and the less educated enter diverging paths. Americans who place less value on education may find themselves in opposition to those with good educations. These lives begin to diverge at an early age. Later on, as their destinies separate, all too often their politics can head in opposing directions. (Much more on causes of educational disparities and their effects on our society in chapter 5.)

Immigration

STATUS: **BOILING**

In a case of amazing cultural amnesia, millions of Americans today oppose any immigration, never mind the illegal one—they even oppose legal immigrants. They have forgotten that they owe their present comforts to their ancestors, who built this unprecedently successful country with courage, self-reliance, postponement of gratification, optimism, and, yes, resilience. Those who oppose immigration confront its supporters. *Gallup* reported on June 21, 2018, that 75% of Americans think that immigration, presumably legal, is a good thing. Of them, 82% were Democrats and 67% Republicans. Illegal immigrants are a subject of discord. Many oppose them vehemently, while others provide them

support unconditionally. Both act from emotional and ideological reasons. The conflicting views fail to address the
country's real need for a legal system of immigration that
serves our requirements. I develop these ideas in chapter 4,
"Immigrants: Agents of Resilience."

Violence and guns

STATUS: **SIMMERING**

On February 22, 2020, a young Black man ran through a
White neighborhood in broad daylight in Brunswick, Georgia.
Two White men saw him run by their house. He thought he was
jogging; they thought he was running. They armed themselves
with a handgun and a rifle, got into their cars, and pursued
him. A third man followed in another car to film them. They
caught up with the Black man, cornered him, and shot him
dead with no provocation at all. The third man filmed it.

This all-too-common episode sums up the dark side of
a divided America: guns, educational deficiency, race, and
cultural lust for violence. We encounter violence at every
turn, a deep-seated American longing found in football,
boxing, fake wrestling, and, supremely, Hollywood movies.
The frontier's inheritance at its worst. Many Americans, of
course, oppose all violence. They confront uncompromising
gun support and its lobby.

For some, guns represent the fantasized male essence
of their Americanness. For others, they provide necessary
tools for violence, ranging from crime to psychosis. But
there is more. *CNN Business* (March 19, 2020) stated, "Gun
sellers across the United States are reporting major spikes
in firearm and bullet purchases as the coronavirus spreads

across the country." As an immigrant, I puzzle. Millions of Americans own firearms with no criminal intent at all. In their interpretation of the Constitution, it is their right. But their adolescent sons can steal their guns and go on a killing rampage in a school, as happened in Colorado and Connecticut, for instance. Or they can have their children play with Daddy's gun and kill another child. CBS (May 20, 2020) reports that every year, some 250 children are thus killed by other minors accidentally.

For other millions of Americans, guns represent a societal and personal threat in need of control and even eradication. Their opponents support the National Rifle Association, an organization so blindly devoted to gun ownership that it finds no objection to the most lethal kind when used for crime and mass shootings. They don't appear to note that in 2020, some twenty thousand Americans were killed with firearms in deliberate acts of violence.[1] No basis for an objective dialogue exists because for some, guns are irreconcilably emotional symbols. I expand on this theme in appendix 3: The Second Amendment and Other Archaic Notions.

Science

STATUS: **BOILING**

Surprisingly, science-related issues such as vaccination, climate change, and even what we teach in schools pack an emotional punch. Two lines of thought collide. One, pre-modern, questions the validity of science because it per-ceives that it undermines closely held political and religious beliefs. The other side pursues preferred social or political objectives that rely on science. A profound discomfort with the effects of accelerating change on one side, a passionate commitment to change on the other, with science as a political cudgel for both. I return in subsequent chapters to the place of science in our changing society.

Race
STATUS: **BOILING**

Many Americans may step gingerly around their views on race, but that issue sits deeply. Racism and antiracism have divided us since the founding of the republic, and legislation furthered by Lyndon Johnson in the 1960s has come nowhere near to resolving it. Prejudice against dark-skinned people has sat deeply in Anglo-Saxon minds for centuries. Now-sainted Winston Churchill said in 1937, "I do not admit that anything wrong has been done to the Redskins of America, nor the blacks of Australia, when a stronger, better quality bred race came and took their place."

And it's not only Anglo-Saxons. Most Whites, whether they admit it or not, share in anti-Black prejudice, some viciously. Between 2008 and 2016, our feelings about race came to a head. We did the theretofore unimaginable: we elected a Black man to the presidency of the United States. Many applauded; others recoiled in horror and resentment. The contrasting, even opposing, electoral campaigns of Obama and Trump describe a racially divided nation.

Ideology and politics
STATUS: **BOILING**

Our ideologies dwell under two very broad umbrellas: conservative and liberal. Each shelters numerous shadings

ranging from extremes to centrist. The two main currents
of thought pivot around how they assess change: much too
fast or not nearly fast or radical enough. Ideology contains
the whole lot: politics, immigration, race, guns, education
and science, nostalgia for an imagined past, and ambitions
of progress. All loudly proclaim our divisions. Particular
acrimony afflicts two pillars of the American identity:
equality and freedom. For some, inequality of wealth, gender,
skin color, and other differences amount to an inequality of access to opportunity and hence limits freedom. For
others, personal freedom from government interference far
outranks equality concerns, at least in political discourse.
Political cable television and social media stoke partisan
divisions. In this feverish climate, politicians fear assuming a
centrist, unifying, nonpartisan, patriotic position.

Environment

STATUS: **BOILING**

Environmental issues, global warming in particular, wear
the mantle of a militant crusade for the more vocal liberal
part of our political spectrum. For that reason, it provokes
uncompromising opposition among its conservative counterparts. The ones fervently assert; the others dismissively deny.
They don't speak to each other. Of course, most Americans
believe in preserving the environment and treating it with
respect. Countless millions visit national parks. Yellowstone
alone attracts some three million annually, Democrats and
Republicans, though there is no way to tell them apart. Their
voices are not heard amid the partisan cacophony. In chapter
8, I propose a balance-of-nature national policy.

Religion

STATUS: **SIMMERING**

The earliest settlers set religion as a cornerstone of their society. First came the Puritans and other Protestants in the North, Catholics in Maryland, and Anglicans in the South. Sects multiplied, but just about everybody went to church on Sundays. Religion held sway. Then came Catholics, Jews, and others and all adhered steadfastly to their religions. But following Darwin came science. With the help of education, it began to peel off religious believers. Now churches stand half-empty, if that—even Black churches, which represent their community. But not those of fundamentalists. They have engaged in education selectively, mostly suspicious of science. Politically, they give stalwart support to the most conservative. Abortion became an ideological splitter. There has been no civil dialogue about abortion for half a century nor about other religion-driven issues. In spring 2021, Southern Baptists, the largest fundamentalist Protestant sect, were experiencing tremors of internal separation along conservative-versus-liberal lines.[2]

Public health

STATUS: **BOILING**

Before the advent of covid-19, public health never caused notable disagreements. Now passions boil between maskers and anti-maskers. Antivaxxers, by rejecting science, made the fight against viruses more difficult. The acerbic politics of the Trump years have brought dormant cultural feelings about public health to the surface.

Flag, anthem, and patriotism

STATUS: **PERCOLATING**

One would think of the flag and the national anthem as unifying symbols of patriotism. One would be mistaken. For a vocal minority, they symbolize oppression, imperialism, colonialism, and other sins. For another vehement minority, the flag functions as a totem for a defiant, rebellious nationalism.

None of the above welcomes dialogue. Yet a national dialogue we badly need, based on facts, data, and respectful listening to those with whom we disagree. Let's consider the potential of that in present-day America.

What unites us

Since this book investigates the resilience of our resilience, I can see no objective, reasoned arguments in support of any of the above divisions, but I see many for our coming together.

E pluribus unum? In light of all the divisions, *unum* would seem elusive. The storms and froth of our disputes, eagerly expanded by calculating or partisan media, would make us doubt that motto. But let's see.

When we step away from the passions that divide our country, we still find that a great majority of individual Americans holds profound shared beliefs. Such beliefs often reside in our cultural instincts rather than in our stated opinions. Let's listen to our language and observe our

personal attitudes and actions that can preserve or invigo-
rate our resilience.

Tolerance

American expressions: "give them a break," "cut them
some slack." The American character is finely attuned to
the fallibilities of human nature and is willing to allow for
redemption from weaknesses and failures. That did not
readily happen in the countries we came from, where centuries of brutal history have honed feelings of irredeem-
able guilt and condemnation. Pardon in those places doesn't
come as easily.

Still, our record of tolerance is limited. At the individual level, it remains reliable. Not so at a collective level.
There, intolerance thrives, largely on the fringes. On the left,
it expresses itself as, "I don't tolerate anyone who doesn't
think like me." On the right as, "I don't tolerate anyone who
doesn't look like me." Our history has shown that it margin-
alizes fringes and hews to the center, where our individual
convictions of tolerance tend to prevail. We'll see how we
perform in these times that test our national character. Can
we unite by personally extending tolerance to all? Which
leads us to . . .

Forgiveness

"There but for the grace of God go I" combines compassion, understanding, and hence forgiveness. We forgive
intuitively because we understand the human condition. In
turn, and logically, this leads us to another American exclusive . . .

Belief in second chances

Even when we don't utter the words "second chances," we understand that they constitute an ingrained conviction in our national character. We practice a belief in second (and more) chances at every turn. They represent a credence that has made America the land of opportunity, where all prospects remain unimpeded by cultural preconceptions about advancement, as is the case in older countries. In that spirit, we favor the underdogs as they are potentially and subconsciously any one of us. It just depends on circumstances, and one never knows when one may need another chance. In that spirit, too, we have legislated in recent decades to open doors to Blacks and others of color to whom, to our shame, we did not offer even first chances in the past.

Among glass-half-empty Americans exists these days the view that second chances have disappeared from our reality.[3] As I mentioned before, the US Census Bureau reported for 2020 that 550,000 new business applications were received, a record by a wide margin (the previous record was 300,000 in 2019). Many among them apparently from resilient individuals who had lost their original businesses to the upheavals caused by the digital economy and covid-19. Belief in second chances is no more?

Embracing challenge

As I say in chapter 2, the word *difficulty* seems to have disappeared from the American vocabulary. We have replaced it with the word *challenge*. Difficulty implies an obstacle and the possibility of failure. Challenge suggests that there will be effort required, but the outcome will clearly end in success. In most Americans' parlance, *challenge* thus unconsciously represents a glass half full: the quintessence of optimism, the stuff that resilience is made of.

Rule of law

"I have my rights," "There ought to be a law"—these expressions are not heard elsewhere. Not surprisingly. The constitutions of democratic France, where I was born, and democratic Switzerland, where I studied, don't include any reference to the rights of the individual. Instead, they proclaim the rights of the state and the duty of the individual to support them. The US Constitution has uniquely made the individual the beneficiary of its legal system. Americans know this intuitively and proclaim it at every turn. We inherited it from England, and it gives us our backbone.

The mob attack on Congress on January 6, 2021, resulted in an affirmation of the rule of the law as responsible individuals in all institutions of government responded unshaken.

Success

Aspiration to success (the American Dream) and the expectation of achieving it are a staple of our culture and a foundation stone of our resilience. The American Dream stands in opposition to resignation and takes for granted the fundamentals shared by the majority: unhindered opportunity, equal protection under the law, freedom from arbitrary coercions, and so forth.

Much pessimistic sentiment, predominantly from the left, proclaims the death of the American Dream along with second chances.[4] In August 2017, the Pew Research Center conducted a survey on the American Dream.[5] It reports that overall, 36% of US adults assert that their family has achieved the American Dream, while another 46% say they are "on their way" to achieving it. That's 82% of Americans. Furthermore, that belief seems spread across ethnicities. Whites, at 41%, are more likely than Blacks, at 17%, or Hispanics, at 32%, to say that they have achieved the American Dream. But more Blacks, at 62%, and Hispanics, at 51%, than Whites, at 42%, state they are on their way to achieving it. Looks like in 2017, most Americans agreed that they can achieve success. Still true after four shocks? In successive chapters, I return to this premise.

Language and culture

The English culture and language have imprinted the American character more than any other influence. All English-speaking persons in our society (well, the immense majority) operate in the realm of that English-imprinted culture. It subtly unifies us. The respect for the rule of the law, the radical concept of a constitution in the eighteenth century, and the Bill of Rights provide the cement that holds our country together, particularly evident in wobbly times like those we have experienced between 2008 and 2021. In America, the easiest way to put an opponent on the defensive is to accuse him of being unfair, a fundamentally English cultural argument. (The essentially English concept represented by the word "fairness" cannot be translated into any other language I know.)

Impulse to help strangers

The great majority of Americans share three behavioral traits: volunteerism, philanthropy, and, less obviously these days, a quest for community. Disregarding politics and other sources of division, Americans respond spontaneously and generously to crises or disasters. Tocqueville noted almost two centuries ago that Americans didn't wait for authorities but took action on their own. "If an accident happens on the highway, everybody hastens to help the sufferer; if some great and sudden calamity befalls a family, the purses of a thousand strangers are at once willingly opened, and small but numerous donations pour in to relieve their distress," Tocqueville wrote in *Democracy in America*.[6] He didn't see this in France, nor would he find it in the rest of Europe.

Volunteering and philanthropizing rise spontaneously from the individualistic American character. For better or worse, we are on our own in this society ("There but for the grace of God"), and we respond unbidden. The numbers may seem fabulous. The National Philanthropic Trust reports that seventy-seven million adult Americans volunteered their time and efforts in 2018—some 30% of the adult population. It also reports that Americans gave some $427 philanthropic billion that year, comparable to the annual gross domestic product of many countries. Argentina, for instance, a nation of forty-five million, had a GPD of $450 billion in 2019.

Fabulous numbers indeed, but a touch of vanity may motivate much hyper-philanthropy when, for instance, seeking entry into the right social circle by supporting the local symphony or donating a college campus building with your name prominently displayed (or when tax-deduction considerations did not escape their attention). The much less fabulous numbers that really matter come from spontaneous responses to human distress in specific crises. Then, more modest numbers more essentially reflect the American character. Let's consider some cases.

A catastrophic fire in November 2018 wiped out the town of Paradise in California's central valley.[7] Its twenty-six thousand people lost nineteen thousand buildings and most of their property, in addition to eighty-five lives. First responders, of course, appeared very quickly and did what they could. But within hours and subsequent days, large numbers of private citizens from towns for miles around came and offered their help. They also donated $114,000 as of May 2019. Millions of dollars were needed, and government agencies supplied most of that, but individuals gave to individual families in gestures of solidarity and support. They didn't ask the victims whether they were Republicans or Democrats, rich or poor. They offered help in a spontaneous impulse of volunteerism and philanthropy.

Hurricane Katrina, which devastated New Orleans and the Gulf Coast in 2005, drew an exemplary amount of private volunteer and philanthropic response. The Corporation for National and Community Service reported estimated numbers in the first year after the catastrophe. It indicates that 575,000 individuals volunteered in person! Additionally, some eighteen million young pope between ages seventeen and twenty-eight donated time and money for relief from Katrina. One assumes that, unbidden, they responded out of an American instinct. Nor that they asked to what race or political party the victims belonged.

That spirit continues. Below are assorted examples from

a Share America report in June 2020.[8] They illustrate the broad range of volunteerism spawned by the covid-19 crisis and how volunteerism has risen once more to its normal American scale:

- At Kaiser Permanente Washington Health Research Institute in Seattle, volunteers participated in the first-stage safety study clinical trial of a potential vaccine for covid-19.

- A nurse traveled from Minnesota to New York to volunteer her help.

- A Hollywood movie executive donated blood to the Red Cross in California.

- At the Hope Community Services in New Rochelle, New York, volunteers packed free groceries for distribution to the elderly.

- A member of a network of volunteers made 3D-printed face shields for emergency service nurses at Harborview Medical Center in Seattle.

- Volunteers built a field hospital at the Cathedral of St. John the Divine in New York.

- Chef Marcus Samuelsson lent his as-yet-un-
  opened Red Rooster Overtown restaurant
  to chef José Andrés's World Central Kitchen
  staff to prepare and distribute meals to those
  in the community affected by the covid-19
  outbreak.

- Monica Cannon-Grant, founder of Violence
  in Boston, helped prepare meals for school-
  children and other community members in
  need at Food for the Soul restaurant in the
  Grove Hall neighborhood of Boston. The
  restaurant and Violence in Boston's Social
  Impact team, in collaboration, fed up to one
  thousand people each day since they began
  offering free meals.

- The Masjid at-Taqwa mosque in the Brooklyn
  borough of New York, closed to worship
  during the covid-19 pandemic, and set up a
  table on its doorstep with packages of bread
  and a crate of apples for passersby.

Whitney Tilson, a wealthy New Yorker and a noted
liberal, volunteered his time and labor to build a field hospital
in New York's Central Park for covid-19 patients. When
asked by his friends why he did it, especially collaborating

with people with whom he strongly disagreed politically and ideologically, he said in essence:

> I was willing to set aside my ideological
> differences because lives were at stake.
> We are truly at war against a ferocious and
> deadly enemy. If the other volunteers and
> I hadn't pitched in, and the hospital hadn't
> opened for an extra two days, what would I
> say to a grieving family who lost a loved one
> who might have been saved? . . . My story
> is one of very different Americans coming
> together under extraordinary circumstances
> and working to fight a common enemy—and
> learning more about one another in the
> process. (email communication)

As we observe ourselves divided these days, let's note and internalize the essentially American meaning of these behaviors. They surround us daily, a theme to which I return in later chapters.

Community spirit

Conceptually, a resilient society consists of resilient individuals. In practice, for resilience to materialize, such individuals must gather around a confident, optimistic community. Resilience is not a solo endeavor. It needs social stimulation.

Throughout history, the neighborly, physical community has stood as a magnet at the center of American life,

attracting newcomers, creating support, and fostering civic
spirit. The typically American communitarian impulse has
led us to develop a word: joinerism. A saying now mostly
disused except in Amish and Mennonite communities
expresses eloquently the American communitarian spirit:
"They helped me raise my barn." Newcomers who formed
a homestead needed a barn, a major construction. When
the time came, the neighbors from surrounding home-
steads gathered to raise the walls of the barn, a day when all
rejoiced.

Helping integrate a stranger into the community has
become a natural social act for most Americans. Though
now reduced in larger cities, it continues on all evidence in
the more traditional heartland. It happened to me. I came to
the United States a penniless immigrant. Kind natives helped
me spontaneously and unbidden to raise my barn, thereby
integrating me into their community and, by extension, into
American society. But in my case, each community turned
ephemeral because I kept moving in quest of opportunity
and a place that suited me. Like me, millions change their
geographic location and come to live in a new community.
But these communities, by now mostly vast, mobile, and
heterogeneous, have largely lost their neighborly feeling.
Therein lies a problem.

In earlier times, in tighter communities, the lawyer, the
doctor, and the minister knew the butcher, the baker, and the
candlestick maker. Not anymore. I live in a community that
resembles me, thinks more or less like me, has a similar level
of education. And we don't know those who live in communities that look, think, or hold opinions in ways that differ

from ours. A country now of many very different communities but reduced national community.

In *Bowling Alone, the Collapse and Revival of the American Community* (2000), sociologist Robert Putnam detected cultural shifts that altered the American community over the past half century.[9] He noted how participation in politics at the individual level diminished significantly and how memberships of voluntary associations like the Rotary, the League of Women Voters, the Knights of Columbus, labor unions, and many other organizations have sagged similarly. Putnam sees many causes, among them a general disillusionment with government but also the advent of technologies with unprecedented capacity to distract and compartmentalize us.

Church attendance and religious identification have also ebbed considerably since the 1970s. The Pew Research Center[10] reports that in the United States, those who identify as Christian have diminished between 2000 and 2018/2019 from 77 to 65% (Protestants from 51 to 43% and Catholics from 23 to 20%), particularly so among urban millennials (born between 1981 and 1996). Though universal and not particularly American, this phenomenon nevertheless reduces in yet another way our physical participation in the community.

American churches, synagogues, and mosques differ, however, from those in other countries. Here, they are more community centers than merely sites of religious practice. While the place of worship may stand at the core of its community, worship may not be its most important feature. In Menlo Park, California, where I live, we have a number of diverse churches. Each may have a school, a community center that provides a range of services for young and old, and other aspects that attract its community. It is the traditional American place where people congregate for a number of social needs and wishes. While church attendance may dwindle, the community around it seems not to have lost its meaning. In their physical continuity, places of worship provide community and social stability.

Contemporary societal changes record a steady departing of individuals from traditional communities. But do resilient communities now form online? Consider Whitney Tilson, above, who joined not necessarily pleasant strangers whom he met online to do what fellow Americans needed. Did these volunteers respond to the greater, tacit, shared community in a crisis? We don't yet know how our society in transition will affect resilience. But covid-19 seeds social changes. The enormous proliferation of Zoom encounters suggests one such prospect. *Forbes* reported in November 2020 that Zoom use had grown by 355% year over year by September 2020.

I belong to an Italian social club in San Francisco. We meet every Thursday for lunch, followed by a speaker on generally an Italian theme. Most members are local and show up in person. We have members in other states whom we actually never see. But Zoom in covid-19 times has replaced our physical encounters, and our members from Arizona, New York, Texas, or southern California join us now. Covid-19 and Zoom are community congregators in a modern world. The form of our communities may evolve, but our community-seeking spirit still seemingly endures.

Of baseball. Let's look at baseball, the repository of so many of our cultural beliefs, particularly of equality and merit. Millions of Americans flow to the ballpark through winter, spring, summer, and fall. In the Baltimore Orioles park, when, during the singing of the national anthem, they reach the line "and our flag was still there," everybody in the stadium turns toward Fort McHenry and points to where the flag still flies. Baseball as ritual assertion of the community.

When the hitter steps up to the plate (a figure of speech in itself), he begins to act out important aspects of American life. He is alone, reliant on self, and being tested. He approaches it as a challenge, in a spirit of optimism and expectation of success. He uses skill and judgment. He is given second and third chances (tolerance and forgiveness). He is also prepared to make sacrifices for his team, his community. Meanwhile, he endures hearty disapproval by fans of the opposing team, testing his resilience. If he hits a homerun, he is rewarded for excellence. If he gets on first base, he has proven himself and now gained the support of his team, his community. He continues to be tested until he reaches home. If he steals a base, he demonstrates daring and risk-taking, qualities we admire. If he fails in his quest for success, there still remain second chances should he step up to the plate in another inning.

> The pitcher, too, benefits from tolerance and for-
> giveness and receives second chances by throw-
> ing three balls. We're human, after all. Meanwhile,
> both pitcher and hitter have the benefit of the rule
> of law as rules apply equally to all players. The
> umpires (the court system) apply them impartially,
> though imperfectly. Of course, being born on third
> base is widely scorned in this country, where
> most of us believe in equality and merit.

We don't find these characteristics in any other sport. So will our cultural resilience bounce back as long as we go to the ballpark?

In this chapter, I've looked at our overt divisions but also at the underlying and enduring currents of shared beliefs that have united us. Which will prevail in changing times? Spanish philosopher Miguel de Unamuno wrote about history riding in the deep subcurrents of *la intrahistoria*. He thought that events are transient but that la intrahistoria—like the deep currents of the ocean as opposed to the passing waves—steadily continues. In the same spirit, I believe/hope that our individually shared cultural beliefs and values—though, at times, tattered by events and by the unscrupulous and irre-sponsible—will carry us back to our fundamental resilience.

In the following chapters, I examine aspects of our culture and components of our society that will determine our future.

Chapter 4

Immigrants: Agents of Resilience

———◆———

That immigrants have built America we accept as a truism, though these days we forget all too often what that truism means. Immigrants laid the foundation of the American character and with that our propensity for optimism and responding resiliently to setbacks. How much of that foundational immigrant culture lives on among most Americans is an essential question about our future. In their great majority, natives descend from immigrants of several generations back. Thus, they have not personally experienced the practice of the immigrant ethic and may have forgotten its essential value. Let's review what that ethic comprises.

- Risk acceptance, ambition for self-improvement and optimism—traits of the courageous, the energetic, and the self-confident who will abandon the certain for the unknown in a quest for a better life.

- Assumption of responsibility for one's actions—no excuses, no one else to blame.

- Self-reliance, because on landing in an alien land, one stands on one's own (and doesn't expect to be bailed out).

- Working hard and postponement of gratification, because the conditions of a new life in a new world impose them.

Adaptability and receptiveness to the new and the unexpected, traits of resilience.

For the majority of first-generation immigrants, the practice of this ethic leads to most often successful lives and translates into enthusiastic patriotism. They take their new citizenship responsibly, vote, and obey laws (mostly).

> Arnold Schwarzenegger arrived young from Austria, little educated and not speaking English. He worked hard, went to college, graduated, and became a citizen, then a famed Hollywood actor, and a German-accented governor of California. In a nutshell.

A vast region, the former Confederate South never received much continued immigration and, with that, not much experience of the correspondent ethic. Immigrants arrived in the North and the West instead, which shapes our politics to this day.

Our national resilience needs constant booster shots of that resilience-building immigrant ethic. Today, legal and illegal immigration presents us with two different but equally important decisions. Let me start with the illegal sort because of its enormous political effect.

Discord among natives

Massive numbers of migrants have crossed our southern border over recent decades, most illegally. They have created adversarial emotions among us. One side opposes illegal immigrants and, to my amazement, also the legal. The other side supports illegal immigrants with fervor, equally to my surprise. In that division, we find yet another subject about which we cannot talk to each other in a civil manner. This doesn't enhance our resilience potential. So here I'll step on a landmine and proceed to probably and regrettably offend, maybe even outrage, many of my readers. I think that both sides are wrong.

I am in sympathy with those who oppose illegal immigrants. Whether they understand it or not, those illicit migrants have come because the law rules here. They came from where the law is easily corrupted. But by entering illegally, they defy the essence of our social contract.

This exasperates many decent, law-abiding, traditional-values-upholding citizens. But the bigots too.

We need to understand opposition to immigrants, legal and illegal, because it carries wider implications for our national discord. That opposition has grown out of resentment of diversity. In the immediate aftermath of John Kennedy's assassination in 1963, an explosion of unexpected forces surfaced in our society, each seeking its place: Blacks, people of other ethnicities or sexual orientations, and women all claimed their spot under the sun of diversity. Legislation in the 1960s recognizing these demands followed, and numerous Whites, men more than women, began to feel that it was all at their expense, an attack on their birthrights and religious beliefs. Beginning in the 1980s, masses of illegal immigrants walked across our southern border into that cultural turmoil. Immigration thus became appended to resentments over diversity, adding another obstacle to a national dialogue.

So much for some sympathy with immigrants' opponents. I break with them when they cast the illegals as criminals, rapists, and welfare abusers. Grossly untrue. Immigrants, even illegal, are largely more law-abiding than the natives. The overall US incarceration rate in 2010 was 3.51 per one hundred thousand. For immigrants, it was 0.68, and even for the most maligned Mexicans, it was 0.70.[1]

The Cato Institute, a libertarian thinktank, has studied immigrants for more than two decades. From a combination of studies, it concludes that illegal immigrants ages eighteen to thirty commit 1.6 crimes per 100,000, whereas American natives of the same age group commit 3.3 crimes by the same

measure. The Cato Institute attributes the low illegal immigrant crime rate to two factors. One is the fear of getting
caught and deported. The other is that they come to the
United States to work, not to commit crimes. In my parlance,
to practice the immigrant ethic. As for welfare abuse, it
depends to whom one listens. Opponents of immigration
claim massive abuse. Defenders of it assert the opposite. It
hinges on how one defines welfare abuse. The dominant fact
is that the law doesn't allow it and that, hence, any government services immigrants receive are legally determined
(surely there are some cheats, given human nature, but persuasive documentation of that is lacking).

And I categorically break with the opponents of immigration when they oppose *legal* immigration, America's
mother milk.

I also find some respect for those supporting illegal
immigrants. (They like to call illegals "undocumented," a
euphemism refusing to admit their illegality, but *undocumented* merely means lacking legal documents, same as
illegal.) Generosity, forgiveness, and compassion are deep-
seated American virtues. We should praise those who
practice them but not when they do it at the cost of the law
in any form. Providing illegals with "sanctuary" cities defies
our laws, and here I break too.

The generosity of our hearts has no right to bypass our
laws. This is a very serious matter. The law cements our
society, as it doesn't in a great many other countries. We
believe in our Constitution, and we follow our laws. Both
can be amended or changed as expressions of the will of our
people. Meanwhile, the law reigns in majesty. The courts

of justice hold our country together, to which we attest by accepting without exception the judicial outcomes, as ex-president Trump has found in suit after suit.

Opponents of illegal immigration and its defenders don't share a common agenda. Opponents view it from a public policy perspective: can the undocumented assimilate culturally, and at what cost to less-educated natives, be they White, Black, or Hispanic? Defenders of the unauthorized don't take a public policy position but rather act from humanitarian feelings. They are largely well-educated metropolitans who disdain their outraged opponents—a situation not conducive to national dialogue. No common ground to address the disagreements?

Well, as I express these views on illegal immigrants, I also note that reality has an insidious way of interfering with theory. I know two ladies.

Adriana came illegally over the border as a young woman from Nicaragua. Isabel also came as a young woman from Mexico, and I haven't asked her how. Both are intelligent, of strong character, and with little formal education. Adriana has raised three daughters in America. All three have master's degrees and married American husbands. She has now American grandchildren of educated parents, with mothers imbued with the immigrant ethic. Isabel raised three sons in this country and put them through college. All three have married young Mexican-American women, and Isabel, too, has American grandchildren of college-educated parents, exposed on both sides to the immigrant ethic.

Both Adriana and Isabel came illegally, actions that I oppose on principle. Both have practiced the immigrant ethic to the fullest. Both work hard to this day; both have assimilated to the degree that first-generation immigrants do. What to make of the results of their assimilation? Do we see an American story here? Possibly something optimistic? Perhaps a smidgen of hope and confidence?

Why we need immigrants now

As we grope toward a new immigration policy that can reduce our discords, we need to ask ourselves: too many of us or not enough? Our population stood in 2021 at 331 million. Our multitudes stress our natural resources, clog freeways, and cause many social and environmental adversities. As we multiply, each of us loses a measure of individuality. We become more anonymous; our neighborhoods lose their community feeling. The antisocial dissolve more easily into invisibility. Government grows as ever larger numbers of us require more services and more attention: more identifying, more control, more laws. All that accentuates our separations.

Yet I advocate for more immigrants. How to justify that? We find ourselves fearful for our health, disunited socially and politically, and with our economy apparently in temporary tatters from a convergence of covid-19, automation, and, for many, e-commerce. Time for immigrants to the rescue. We need them for economic vitality, we need them to boost health services and our scientific research, we need them to rejuvenate us demographically, but, mostly, we need them to revitalize our culture by injecting a solid shot of immigrant ethic.

The economy needs them

Once the large unemployment caused by covid-19 subsides, immediate critical shortages of skilled labor will surface.

On September 17, 2014, the Conference Board, an independent business think tank, released a study, *From Not Enough Jobs to Not Enough Workers.*[2] It details categories of skilled labor where we fall well short of our needs. Most of these jobs require training and education of less than a bachelor's-degree level. They include, among numerous technical activities, mechanics, boilermakers, crane and tower operators, transportation workers, water and waste operators, and specialized clerical positions. The reasons for these shortages are manifold. Our education system doesn't produce enough of them. Too many young choose college over training for well-paying technical skills. We have lowering birth rates and hence fewer young people seeking jobs. A generation of older skilled workers is retiring, and their work doesn't seem appealing to those seeking a college education.

The Bureau of Labor Statistics echoes these conclusions in 2021. It projects upward of six million new jobs formed in the 2020s. Many will require technical skills and scientific knowledge beyond a high-school diploma.[3] For these conditions we are unprepared, and even at this writing millions of skilled jobs go begging in the United States.[4] Our native resources are insufficient. We need this category of immigrants to step in.

But we also need large numbers of low-skilled and hence low-paid manual workers, predominantly in a wide range of service activities such as restaurant work, municipal services, and essential agriculture. Natives mostly find such jobs unappealing. A certain category of immigrants may feel otherwise. Of the unskilled we will need millions too.

Importantly, we have a never-ending want for risk-embracing entrepreneurs, revitalizers of the economy, who create multitudes of jobs and invest in growth. Here, the immigrants stand out. Think about immigrant Elon Musk. He has infused into the economy PayPal, Tesla automobiles, SpaceX rockets, and spacecraft. Admittedly, an exceptional individual but far from alone. The National Foundation for American Policy reports that as of October 1, 2018, 55% of one-billion-dollar startups had at least one immigrant founder. Of the forty-one Fortune 500 companies created since 1985, eight had an immigrant founder. Looks like the American Dream may be alive in immigrant quarters. *Forbes* (July 19, 2019) reported that immigrant entrepreneurs account for 25% of all new businesses in the United States ("Immigrant Entrepreneurs Prove It Doesn't Matter Where You Were Born").

Of course, we need an unending supply of brains, the best we can produce or find, for the economy and for society generally. We fall short of high-grade engineers and of theoretical and applied scientists and researchers.[5] To retain our leadership in the twenty-first century, we need to import brains, and here immigrants remain a crucial resource. Of the 122 Americans who won a Nobel Prize between 2000 and 2018, thirty-four were immigrants. Four of the five Americans who won Nobels in 2016 were born outside the country. Brains come to America because we encourage free, unconventional thinking; we fund it and support it.

Health services need them too

As in the general economy, our health services also fall considerably short of their personnel needs. The *AMN Healthcare* newsletter projected in 2016 the needs of medical personnel over the following decade, to 2026, as follows:

- 1,260,000 *additional* healthcare positions, of which

- 882,000 are diverse clinical support and lab technicians,

- 204,000 certified nurses,

- 52,000 therapists,

- 30,000 physicians and surgeons, and

- 29,000 physician assistants.

Our educational system at its various levels has been unable to produce sufficient numbers of these professionals and is not likely to in the foreseeable future. Consequently, here, too, immigrants need to fill voids.

Some 150,000 certified, highly valued, caring Philippine nurses currently work in the United States.[6] Can the Philippines send us ninety-five thousand more? Russia, Eastern Europe, India, and Latin America produce some qualified health technicians and professionals. Our immigration policy should invite them. They will not take any

American jobs and thus not contribute to further discord between us (except perhaps by irritating those suspicious of foreign accents).

Demography

So we need immigrants to fill all the needs that we cannot address on our own. We know their rough numbers. Still, we also need immigrants for another reason: to redirect our fertility trends, which lag severely below a replacement rate. In demographic terms, *fertility* refers to the actual production of offspring and is measured by the number of births in a year divided by the number of women aged fifteen to forty-four, divided by 1,000. A *population replacement rate* refers to the number of children a couple needs to produce to replace itself. That number is 2.1 children per woman. The United States is nowhere near that (desirable) level, and, furthermore, our fertility is dropping.[7] The National Center for Health Statistics reports in 2020 that our overall fertility rate is at 1.7 births per woman, at 1.6 for White mothers, 2.0 for Hispanic mothers, and 1.8 for Black mothers. None sufficient to produce enough young to maintain the vigor of our society and our economy. Yet a society without a constant inflow of young loses spiritual buoyance indispensable for psychic resilience.

We need to reverse this trend. If we don't, we will suffer the consequences. This will result in a loss of youthful energy and enthusiasm, inventiveness, and innovation—all that fuels resilience. An aging population doesn't stimulate these qualities in its society.

In a report in 2010, the Population Reference Bureau

explains what happens to countries whose population falls below the replacement rate.[8] In Italy, the working-age population will shrink by 20% between 2005 and 2035 and a further 15% by 2050. In Japan, the twentysomething workforce, its best educated ever, will have dwindled by a fifth in the decade ending in 2030. Much of the northern hemisphere, including most of Europe, Russia, China, and South Korea, faces these conditions.

The shrinking pool of their working-age populations has become a drastic problem for these countries. In addition to losses of skills and knowledge, the most harmful effects descend on those older than sixty-five. Low birth and fertility rates jeopardize pension guarantees and long-term healthcare programs for retirees. State pension systems face difficulties now, when in some countries four people of working age remain to support each retired person. By 2030, Japan and Italy will have only two per retiree; by 2050, the ratio will be three to two. Worldwide in 1950, twelve individuals of working age labored for every person over sixty-five. By 2010, that number had shrunk to nine. By 2050, it is projected to drop to two.[9]

Aggravating these trends, medical breakthroughs continue to raise life expectancy in all industrialized countries. The European Commission estimates that demographic changes may push up public spending by between 5 and 8% of the gross domestic product by 2040. Taxpayers will resist footing that bill. An aging, shrinking population poses problems in other surprising ways. The Russian army has had to tighten up conscription because of a shortage of young men.

All this can happen to us. Without the addition of particular kinds of legal immigrants, US fertility will not reach the 2.1 replacement rate in the foreseeable future. The Center for Immigration Studies supplies the data for table 4.1, which shows how the fertility rate of immigrants exceeds that of American native-born, in some respects considerably, and how the level of education plays a decisive role.

Table 4.1
Fertility rates of US native-born and of immigrants[10]

	Fertility rate
US high-school dropouts	2.3 children
US college graduates	1.8 children
Immigrants lacking a high-school degree	3.3 children
Immigrant college graduates	1.9 children

Table 4.1 highlights the direct relationship between education and fertility. Both less-educated native-born and immigrants have higher fertilities than their college-educated counterparts. So should our fertility requirements discourage both high-school completion and college education? The longer-term trends in the fertility of native-born citizens appear destined to decline from their current 1.7 rate in any case. Can immigrants continue to push our fertility rate up to the desirable 2.1 replacement level? If we attract less-educated immigrants, this should help keep our demographic trends in balance. Even that is uncertain because the latest projections suggest declining birth rates among immigrant mothers.

Data in Table 4.1 create a dilemma when we try to craft
a new and better immigration policy. To add another com-
plication, in addition to education level, we need to consider
national origin. Table 4.2 includes potential newcomers from
a range of non-European countries. They are our future
population, as they are already California's now. Table
4.2 describes how their fertility evolves once they settle in
America.

Table 4.2
Immigrant fertility rates in the United States[11]

Country	Fertility rate in home country	Fertility rate in United States
Mexico	2.40	3.51
Philippines	3.22	2.30
China	1.70	2.28
India	3.07	2.23
Vietnam	2.32	1.70
Korea	1.23	1.57
Cuba	1.61	1.79
El Salvador	2.80	2.97
Canada	1.51	1.86
United Kingdom	1.86	2.84
Total fertility rate of sending countries	2.32	2.86

After settling in the United States, the total fertility rate
of sending countries rises to 2.86. Very encouraging when
compared with the current 1.70 rate of the native-born (rates

in table 4.2 are, however, trending lower as prosperity rises across the board).

Though most new entrants come from countries with higher fertility rates than America's, not all do. Filipinos, Vietnamese, and Indians show decreasing fertility rates upon settling in the United States. They are also, on average, the best educated. For the other national groups, planting roots in America increases their fertility rate. Most generally come from economically, socially, or politically unfavorable conditions. Not only does such provenance discourage childbearing, but it also curtails education. In consequence, they arrive much less schooled than Filipinos, Vietnamese, and Indians but much more prone to bear children. Education versus fertility again. (Brits and Canadians would seem the curious exceptions.)

No simple answers. Let's revisit Adriana and Isabel, whom I described above. Each created three children: birth rates of 3.0—a good boost to our fertility rate. Furthermore, all six children finished college, and three achieved a master's degree. All six, now married, are producing little Americans. Is this a typical story? Unusual? Exceptional? I suspect it is uncommon because children of immigrants, now American natives themselves, engender lower birth rates.

Yes, but can they bring us the immigrant ethic?

I stand solitary among swirling crowds on a Manhattan corner, knowing no one to talk to. This is the dominant memory of my first few weeks as an immigrant in the United States. Unsure, unable to recognize where my next pennies would come from or what my future held, I had no one to rely upon but myself. A typical immigrant, like many millions before me. Nonetheless, I had no doubt about America. I knew from observation and intuition that here one cannot fail (success is, of course, how each of us defines it). The natives treated me with pleasant informality instead of a formalistic bureaucracy like I found in every country where I had lived until then. They judged me only by what I could do. I met the psychological and cultural conditions of the frontier, as have most immigrants, even after the physical frontier had disappeared.

Experiences like mine have been the rule for generations of newcomers. From its beginnings, America made Americans out of those migrants regardless of their origins. The English landed first; then came Germans in the eighteenth century, and Benjamin Franklin didn't want them. They stayed, and so did many Hessian soldiers whom the British brought to fight the Americans during the Revolutionary War. The Hessians weren't going back to Westphalia, where they would be poor and not free. They understood the potential of America. The Germans gave us Eisenhower and Nimitz, Bausch and Lomb, not to mention famous beers. Then came the Scots-Irish in that same century. Eastern Pennsylvanians pushed into Appalachia, and they stayed, procreated, enriched our culture musically, and produced a few presidents.

Then Famine Irish came in the nineteenth century and were treated by many natives with the hostility reserved for Hispanics these days. But they, too, stayed and provided three presidents for the United States. Later in the nineteenth century came Eastern and Southern Europeans, and they also integrated into the prevailing Anglo-Saxon culture. Among them came Jews, and we know what happened: a cascade of Nobel Prizes in the sciences, economics, and literature from their descendants. And George Gershwin and Aaron Copland, who wrote the essential American music. Later in the twentieth century arrived Asians and Latin Americans and even some Africans. Most were legal, and they integrated. Muslims, ever more numerous, have assimilated and prospered. As for those who came illegally over our southern border, they are a work in progress, but here I refer again, a little reluctantly, to the stories of Adriana and Isabel.

All practiced the immigrant ethic, most honorably. Most became Americans. Can all this still happen today?

A few of those earlier immigrants went back, but then that was difficult economically and psychologically. Conditions in the twenty-first century are quite different. Air travel and all other transportation forms are easy and cheap. The skilled and the educated among potential immigrants are not poor. They have anchors in their home countries, now prosperous and even democratic. They may have two passports, one of which is American for convenience. Their motivation will reflect the conditions of this century. The United States for our future immigrants may become only a choice, not a destination or one's destiny. Will they feel a cultural and political commitment to the United States as I did?

The power of the American Idea, equality before the law and unimpeded opportunity in an environment of personal liberty, transformed earlier immigrants into committed Americans. It remains uncertain whether those who will come next will have the instinct to become fully assimilated.

None of this, to our dishonor, applies to those brought in bondage and against their will from Africa. The miracle of the American Idea is that despite being mistreated and discriminated against, as they were and still are, many actually and honorably practice the immigrant ethic. Most are proud Americans. Amazing! Isabel Wilkerson in *The Warmth of Other Suns* (2020) movingly and eloquently describes their plight and their American history.[12]

An immigration policy acceptable to all

Immigrants constructed this nation; let's not forget it. We need to reestablish a civil and informed dialogue among all citizens on this essential aspect of our identity. For that, the United States needs a new, well-thought-out, multipartisan immigration policy. It must replace the current helter-skelter, arbitrary rules that hamper us. For instance, in 2019, there was a bureaucratic backlog of nearly four million individuals whose immigration petitions had been approved but who had not yet been admitted. Canada, meanwhile, poaches skilled immigrants who want to come to the United States but whom our policies prevent from obtaining visas. They migrate to Canada instead.[13]

We know in broad outline whom we need and roughly

in what numbers. But questions remain. What do we want these future immigrants to bring: knowledge, skills, labor, fertility, but also enduring commitment to our society and citizenship? Preferably all of that, of course, because those are the ingredients of our resilience. But a new immigration policy will have to consider tradeoffs and complexities.

That some of us believe we need immigrants doesn't mean that most agree. In this chapter, I discuss the cleavage between us on this subject. But even among those who agree, different opinions exist. Between the economy and our health services, our need for skilled and educated immigrants amounts to about ten million in the next decade, allowing for an annual attrition of 1.5 million.[14] While the skilled and educated seem indispensable, they may not contribute to the resilience of our society. In the present social, economic, and cultural configuration of the world, they may not wish to stay, found families, commit to citizenship, and hence bring us all the advantages of an enduring immigrant ethic. They may view their working years in the United States as temporary and return to their countries after a certain period. The less-educated manual workers, on the other hand, are more likely to stay, found families, become citizens, add an immigrant ethic, and thus enhance our resilience. Here again I think of Adriana and Isabel and of the tradeoffs before us. Hence:

The new policy

- It needs to stipulate *our needs* as the sole criterion for legal admission. No illegal admission, of course. The factors I describe above

would determine specific numbers and
qualifications.

- It should *reconsider present policies.* For
instance, how does allowing family members
to join their immigrant relatives already in
the country serve our needs? They amount
to over one million annually, almost 70% of
those currently admitted to settle lawfully in
the United States.[15] This policy adds to our
331 million. What else does it add?

- It should provide for *refugees,* rigorously
defined as such. Our generous country of
millions of volunteers and philanthropists
must find a place in our midst for those
who flee brutal, life-threatening regimes.
There should be no quotas for refugees, and
policy should reflect circumstances. But our
national honor (what an old-fashioned idea!)
will be affirmed if we create room for them
as a matter of heart and policy.

- It should prohibit and penalize *birth tourism,*
as when a pregnant mother arrives in the
United States with the sole purpose of giving
birth because our present law automati-
cally makes that child a US citizen. There is

obviously no advantage to us in this infringe-
ment of the spirit of our existing policy.

- It must reform our *consular service,* mostly
  understaffed, not reputed for efficiency, and
  curiously bureaucratic. For instance, at the
  US consulate in Buenos Aires, when I applied
  for immigration papers, the questionnaire
  asked whether I planned to assassinate the
  president of the United States. It left me
  puzzled, but I prudently answered in the
  negative. Our consular employees need to be
  trained to make savvy decisions about how
  many and which skilled and educated and
  how many less-educated to admit. Our con-
  sulates in Mexico and Central America could
  go a long way to mitigating the problem of
  illegal crossings of our southern border.

It needs to consider the influence of immigrants' taxes
on Medicare and Social Security programs. Taxes of well-
paid professional and skilled immigrants will support both
programs in higher proportion than those of less-educated,
low-paid immigrants. The latter will draw on both programs
in a higher proportion in older age. Of immigrant-headed
households, 51% receive some form of lawful social assis-
tance in any given year (as opposed to only 30% of native
households).[16] A well-considered policy will seek a balance.

I hope that the case for our needing immigrants persuades. How to convert it into political reality is the task. We need to talk to each other, especially to those categorically opposing immigration. A daunting challenge today but necessary to meet if we want to bolster our resilience.

Chapter 5

Education: Our Struggle against Low Expectations

———————◆———————

Well-developed, agile minds respond resiliently.

Cleavage on immigration, cleavage in education too. Resilience, let's remember, stems from optimism and confidence that coalesce around a shared, robust civic and political center. Present profound differences in education among Americans prevent us from achieving that goal. The educated vote primarily for one party, the less so predominantly for the other. The educated garner information—and, hence, facts and data—from various sources. The less so from few, if any. The ones read much, the others hardly at all. The ones watch frivolity on TV, the others don't. This engenders incomprehension and disdain for each other. The exact opposite of what our national interest requires.

The resolution of this state of affairs demands at least a comparable level of education for all Americans, with a comparable comprehension of the modern world. In simpler times, educational differences would not have mattered as much. Appendix 2 shows, however, that in simpler times, our public education was better than today. Science and knowledge define our times, and differences in education now influence the course of our society. Such conditions require much more and better instruction for all and more steeply for those lagging.

In our present world, I cannot muster a rational argument in favor of ignorance or for the low-information voter. Knowledge is to me an absolute, indisputable good. Our national interest requires that we make good education *for all* our priority. This objective faces three obstacles:

1) a culture in which, for many, knowledge seems to count for little;
2) a society in which millions of children start life against seemingly unsurmountable educational handicaps; and
3) an antiquated structure of our elementary- and secondary-school system that fails many millions of our young.

These towering obstacles, often combined, stand in the way of our achieving a more harmonious and more resilient society. None can be overcome quickly. We can achieve some relatively fast progress through enlightened social policy that addresses disadvantaged conditions in our society and by drastic improvements in our educational system. To that end we need to commit ourselves now. Deeper progress can result only from generational replacement over a longer term—a process of successive generations changing their values as a reflection of their evolving culture.

Our culture

Let's examine our culture as an impediment to our education. A main objective of our public education system aims to produce citizens able to responsibly participate in the civic affairs of their country and to share a common culture.

We are an undereducated nation, where being undereducated carries no shame. I know college graduates who don't know why Mexicans speak Spanish, or where Morocco is, or who Teddy Roosevelt was. It's our culture. Generations of undereducated migrants arrived on our shores. As long as they worked productively and behaved as cooperative members of their community, their level of education mattered little. Being overeducated was not always viewed favorably either. Lyndon Johnson, president, referred to Senator William Fulbright as "that overeducated son of a bitch." A culture of low educational expectations.

In my first firm job in America, I taught languages at a small Catholic college in Pennsylvania. One day at lunch in the faculty lounge, the college librarian, of all people, pronounced, quite self-satisfied, these startling words: "I haven't read a book in twenty-five years, and here I am." I had lived in the United States for some six months by then, and those words stunned me. But over the succeeding decades, I came to see that this man represented a solid branch of the American cultural tree. Millions of college graduates like him see no value in education per se. They got a credential, and it suffices.

In fact, one statistic informs us that in 2015, some 27% of American adults hadn't read a book of any kind that year.[1] I suspect that this is an undercount and also that such individuals evince no interest in new knowledge, thoughts, or information in any case. This indifference to education sits deeply in the character of many Americans, whose immigrant ancestors may have sought to acquire skills sufficient for a successful material life but not more.

Of course, this absence of desire for adaptive self-improvement runs counter to the needs of our times. Not all who avoid self-education suffer material consequences. Some may dwell in low-paying jobs, but others conduct well-remunerated lives from their skills or even from professional training. Nevertheless, they harm us all by not participating in the national discourse at a well-informed level that a modern society requires. Especially worrisome is the mindless interaction with social media by millions of the less educated. They uncritically absorb untruths, conspiracy theories, and malign trivia or, worse, Russian misinformation that sabotages our elections. All going viral, all impediments to a national dialogue.

Russian friends ask me how often Americans speak of or seek information about Russia (apparently hostile Russian TV is obsessed with the United Sates). I tell them never—and not only about Russia but any other country. Of course, I add, there is a tiny minority of sophisticated Americans who know and care about the outside world, but the overwhelming majority of our citizenry has no intellectual curiosity. It's a cultural trait.

Fully repairing this gap between the educated and those less so has no immediate correction. In 1960, 90% of the students I taught were first-generation college attendees with scarcely educated parents. Today, their grandchildren may mostly go to college as part of a multigenerational replacement process that will in time overcome indifference to knowledge deemed "unneeded." As of now, intelligent policy can accelerate this evolution of our culture, as I discuss below in the section on our schools.

Our children

Preparing **all** children's brains for the learning experience constitutes a national priority. Let's consider the brain development of our children. Neurological research informs us that children's brains develop very rapidly from birth onward and are extremely receptive to stimulation.[2] Brains of children of well-educated, caring families generally receive an abundance of favorable stimuli from birth on: exposure to rich vocabulary, music, elementary counting. They reach their schooling years with a huge capital of verbal knowledge. That smooths their educational paths into lives of prospective success. From birth, they are likely headed into the educated stratum.

The opposite happens to brains of children born into

unfavorable conditions. Such conditions include poverty, with all the attendant disadvantages. These brains suffer from absence of abundant stimulation because of parental ignorance, absence, or indifference. These handicaps don't only hamper most children in poverty. Better-off families can be equally damaging through parental cultural indifference to education. Homes without books. Homes without conversation. We can find all these conditions in the United States in any racial or ethnic environment. These children arrive into the educational system greatly in arrears when compared to those with well-developed brains. They enter a life of obstacles.

Earliest exposures thus may separate Americans at birth. Our children can even then become tracked into two different directions that prefigure the divisions of our society. A study in 2007 reports that by age three, the observed cumulative vocabulary for children in professional families was 1,116 words; for working-class families, it was about 740, and for welfare families 525.[3] Such data, of course, counter our national interest, which calls for all our children to converge toward a broadly common level of knowledge. We need to chip away at these differences relentlessly and methodically. In chapter 8, under "An education policy," I propose specifics.

But in clouded skies perhaps a sunbeam. *The Economist* (October 3, 2020, "The rugrat race") reports an unexpected trend. In the United States and other countries, "thinly" educated, largely poor mothers have begun to follow practices of well-educated, more affluent mothers. By increasing the time they spend with their little ones and in providing them intensifying mental stimuli, these less-educated mothers aim to raise their children toward a more ambitious future. If this trend gains momentum, we can expect more comparably developed brains in children from all strata of our society when they reach elementary school. What causes this welcome trend? Much as social media can diffuse the inane or the dangerous, nothing is hidden anymore, and I suspect that in this case, good parental practices have also spread through the internet.

Whatever cultural disadvantages may afflict a given group, the consequences should not have a lifelong effect. A prevailing school of thought maintains that the crucial brain development years are zero to three. Current neurological research demonstrates that this view is too restrictive and that the brain keeps evolving and adapting throughout our lives.[4] We can overcome disadvantages by constant brain stimulation.

> For several years, my wife, Mimi, headed Concerts for Kids, a program sponsored by the Mid-Peninsula League of the San Francisco Symphony. To save money, the State of California has canceled music teaching in public schools. To compensate, Mimi and other musically trained members of the league volunteered at schools in East Palo Alto and East Menlo Park, California, two economically and culturally deprived communities. The league volunteers teach fundamentals of music, instruments, melodies,

and ideas of composition to second-, third-,
and fourth-grade children. In the spring of
the academic year, the league volunteers
pack the children into several buses and
take them to Davis Hall, in San Francisco, for
a symphonic concert. Most of these children
had never been in San Francisco, thirty
miles distant, nor seen its splendid City
Hall or attended a cultural event. We don't
know for how many children this may have
become a transformational experience. But
we do know that multiple new impressions
develop the brain. Concerts for Kids has
operated for a number of years and continues to this day.

What do we take away from this? The league volunteers
expose the children to some, not much, music. More significantly, the children's brains absorb abundant stimuli, not
available in their family or scholastic environments.

On a personal observation, I don't know whether I
received from birth the recommended dose of brain stimulation, but due to fateful family circumstance, I found myself
speaking four languages at age six: Russian, French, Serbian,
and German. I didn't know that I spoke those languages. My
brain simply retrieved words appropriate to each situation.
Only later did my mother explain that I spoke languages.
Circumstances of life forced my brain, at the advanced age
of six, to perform new mental acrobatics, a task for which
it was prepared. I believe that this had incalculable positives for the rest of my life. As I navigated through the shoals

of the unexpected and the unfamiliar, my brain seemed prepared to find the right responses from what it had heard and retained.

Jennifer Doudna, an American biochemist, received the Nobel Prize in chemistry in 2020. In *The Codebreaker, Jennifer Doudna, Gene Editing and the Figure of the Human Race*, Walter Isaacson, her biographer, describes her childhood in a small town in Hawaii, where she attended an undemanding school. She had a father, however, who fed her books from earliest childhood and took her on nature observation walks. She probably excelled in her studies because she had been intensely intellectually stimulated by her college-professor parents.

Challenging mental adventures benefit children's brains when prompted early and often. Far-reaching policy should promote steps to locate needy children and provide them with an ample menu of mental stimuli. We should also be wary of the abovementioned, popularized theory that by age three our brains are basically formed and our destinies therefore sealed. Ours is the land of infinite chances. The brains of our young should seize them at any age, at any opportunity, and certainly during their schooling. New brain synapses grow throughout our lives.

Our schools

So, because of the circumstances of their upbringing, our children's brains arrive in schools unequally prepared for learning. Yet the purpose of the schooling years is to prepare citizens uniformly knowledgeable at a certain essential level. Let's see how well we're doing. I have elected to speak about our high-school results because we have measurable data, which we don't for lower grades.

In my 2018 book, *We're 34th in Education!*, I examine why too many American fifteen-year-olds find themselves far behind peers in other advanced countries. The data for that book came from the Program for International Student Assessment (PISA), the most prestigious and influential of such programs. It tests some 3.2 million fifteen-year-olds triennially across seventy-nine countries and regions in math, science, and reading. PISA data for 2012, released in 2014 (the most recent at that writing), showed the United States thirty-fourth in the world. We ranked thirty-sixth in math, twenty-eighth in science, and twenty-fourth in reading. Data for 2018 indicate improvement in reading but not in mathematics or science.

PISA data shouldn't surprise us. American College Testing indicated that in 2012, only 64% of graduating high-school students met the benchmark standard in English, 44% in reading and in math, and 36% in science.[5] National Assessment of Education Progress data for 2015 support it. That year, only 25% of graduating seniors rated proficient in math and averaged 287 on a scale of 500 in reading.[6] What does a high-school credential mean?

But we spend billions on education! To be exact, $739.6 billion in 2016/2017 for elementary and secondary public education among federal, state, and local expenditures. And this is what we get for our money?[7]

Well, it is actually quite difficult to deliver education of an even quality across the United States. In Europe and other parts of the world, a national Ministry of Education issues a national curriculum for all the schools. Not so in America, which differs in this respect also. Here, every community expresses its educational ideas through its schools. We have some 26,400 public high schools. This means that each of some twenty-six thousand communities has an individual education policy reflecting local social and cultural conditions. They educate in their public schools some 15.4 million students yearly. To complicate policies and outcomes, some ethnic groups do better than others. Asian students graduate at a 92% rate, Whites at 89%, Hispanics at 81$, and Blacks at 79% (2018 data). None of this applies to private high schools, which follow their own guidelines and educate about 1.7 million students.

We have some, not many, absolutely excellent public and private schools, on par with the best in the world. Unfortunately, this excellence by and large escapes our notice, submerged as it is in the vast mediocrity of the vast majority of our public schools. Let's begin with what's good in our education and promising for our future.

The good. Two programs account for most outstanding results in our public and private high schools: advanced placement (AP) and the international baccalaureate (IB). To remain a leading force in a knowledge-based world, or at least competitive, we need to value and greatly expand both of these programs.

In 2017–2018, American public high schools offered some twenty-two thousand AP programs, to an extent. Almost 2.9 million students took at least one AP course that year.[8]

Impressive numbers, but the reality is much more limited. In the great majority of cases, students had taken only a couple AP courses, which may have enhanced only some of their college readiness.[9] Only 40,600 (out of 15.4 million), however, had completed the full AP capstone program in 2018.[10] Sadly, IB, the gold standard in American education, recognized by the best universities in the world, also shows similar small numbers. In 2020, only 942 IB programs operated, many at private high schools, and they taught only a few thousand students in the United States. These data give a measure of the restrained reach of these two high-aspirations programs.

The schools where the best of our public education takes place are also few. The universal measure adopted by American high schools is college readiness, with 100 as the maximum score. It is calculated by various criteria, ACT and SAT tests being until 2019 the most influential. States differ somewhat in the accepted criteria. If measured by college readiness, only thirty-two *public* high schools out of some 26,400 exceeded 90.0 in readiness. In 2016, they taught 22,579 students out of 15.4 million—a mere 0.146%. These few outstanding schools are all free but selective, and most are either charter or magnet schools. They attract the best teachers and are financed partly by their states and largely by massive philanthropy. Of these thirty-two schools, fourteen attained a full 100 in college readiness in 2016. A considerably larger number of better private schools, though still not many, provides another dollop of quality education.

Public charter and magnet schools play a most important role. Though selective, they are free and accept students from all strata of their community, including from poorest families and low-education parents, as long as the students adhere to the discipline and the regulations of the school. Most, not all, charters and magnets deliver disproportionately high results of college readiness. Some very successful charters are organized as chains of several schools, all following the same standards, among them KIPP in New York and Summit in California and Washington State.

From this welter of data and information emerge some conclusions. The painfully low extent of our educational excellence should shock us. Nor would it even exist without very extensive, mostly local or community-based philanthropy. What excellence we have creates a potential elite and does not represent our society as a whole. It thus contributes to separations in our country and paradoxically, through its very excellence, undermines the consensus on which our resilience depends. None of that should, of course, discourage us from vastly and energetically expanding the reaches of our educational ambition. The goal is not to level down but to level up.

The not so good. Beneath this very thin layer of highest quality, we begin to find some reasons why we are thirty-fourth. A few dozen public high schools still deliver strong results. The best score between 85.0 and 89.9 in college readiness, very good; but the lowest achieve about 50.0, hardly acceptable. All produce some excellent students but also increasingly more mediocre ones the lower one descends the college-readiness scale.

A model in this range is Walnut Hills High School in Cincinnati, Ohio's best public high school. Neither charter nor magnet, it is a traditional school with nearly 2,400 students. It defines itself as college pre- paratory and has a rigorous curriculum. Better than four out of five seniors rate col- lege-ready, despite such presumed handi- caps as 33% Black students and 21% disad- vantaged. Mainstream and disadvantaged students score equally in proficiency, which stands at 94% in reading and 97% in math- ematics. Ninety-two percent of students attempt AP college-readiness tests, and 85% pass. Overall, it delivers 81.3 in college readiness (all 2016 data).

If only our average high schools were that good! How does Walnut Hills achieve it? It's *parents + community + money* interacting. On the school's website, "Parents" occupy the first and uncommonly extensive position. The WHHS Parent Association incorporates parents, teachers, and community in a joint effort to support and improve the school. The association raises $300,000 yearly. The Cincinnati Board of Education lends it strong support (community in the broader sense). The school is open to all adolescents in the city, provided they can pass a demanding admission test.

There is much to consider here. What in that community's culture produces such exemplary achievement? What if all American high schools performed like this school? Why can't they? How different might our nation look if all could? (Not all programs, of course, need be college preparatory, but all need to aim for excellence.)

The not good at all. Beneath this very-good-to-middling group, we descend into the abyss of some twenty-six thousand high schools (out of 26,400) where none reach even 50.0 in college readiness. That's 98.4% of our public high schools! In one state (North Dakota), the best school reports 0.0% in college readiness. In the lower reaches of this universe, AP and IB programs do not appear. Some such communities may value their high school more for achievements on the football field than for the college scholarships attained. In America, in the twenty-first century. This critical situation has incalculable consequences for our future. Why aren't we massively upset across the land?

What's the reason?

Many of our schools may have fine teachers and excellent facilities, but we need to ask why most school boards would not aim for or be capable of achieving excellence. Our public schools express the values and priorities of their communities. When expressions of local culture shortchange education, they detract from our national resilience—dependent as it is on a shared civic discourse. So if Cincinnati can do it at Walnut Hills High School, which embodies the cultural commitment of its community, why can't we do it across the nation? Let's consider another high school that represents much of the current state of our culture and the diversity of our communities.

> Menlo-Atherton High School (M-A) sits in a very prosperous corner of California's Silicon Valley. It has a splendid campus, an excellent academic program, outstanding laboratory equipment with the most modern technology, a highly qualified faculty (twenty-two math teachers), a remarkable auditorium, and superb athletic facilities. It offers eighteen AP courses and produces some fifty national merit scholars at different levels. Yet it scores 41.4 in college readiness (2016 data), compared with 81.3 at Walnut Hills.

> Its student body of two thousand draws from Menlo Park and Atherton, where most parents are well educated and many affluent, and from East Menlo Park, with poorer and less-educated parents. This results in an ethnically diverse student body: 41% White, 40% Hispanic, 7% Asian, and 5 percent Black; the disadvantaged amount to 31% (2017 data).

> Parents at M-A appear very involved. They

support a foundation that raises considerable money for academics, including
improved teachers' salaries and computer
technology. Thanks to the foundation,
all students, advantaged and disadvantaged, have school and home access to the
internet. In addition, parents participate as
athletics, band, and drama boosters. So why
the 41.1 college readiness?

A closer look shows why. M-A's academic
performance index stands at 822 (on a scale
to 1,000). Pretty good, but only 43% of the
students take AP tests, and they score a fine
952. The rest, most of whom do not take AP
tests, score an exceedingly modest 669. The
school boasts a large career and technology
program, but those most likely to benefit
from it need to score much higher than 669
in proficiency.

M-A features the contradictions of our public educational
system. It encompasses the advantaged, the mainstream,
and the disadvantaged. It can deliver very good academic
results. Every year, it has several semifinalist National Merit
Scholars and National Merit Hispanic Scholars. So why do
57% not attempt AP tests? Who are they?

Here is a clue. M-A boasts a hall of fame. It is not about
academic prowess. The central corridor in the school's
administration building is lined with photographs of M-A's

most glorious athletes over many years—dozens and dozens of them, boys' and girls' swimming, water polo, soccer, tennis, lacrosse, and, of course, football. But one will *not* find any photos of the school's National Merit or other distinguished scholars. Or even of the school's fine orchestra. This corridor discloses an insight into much of our culture's opinion of education: socialization through fun first, study (distant) second.

How to improve on 41.4 college readiness? Money perhaps? M-A benefits from its community's high property taxes. Its foundation raises additional funds. Money doesn't seem to be the problem here. What do the splendid athletic facilities, which cost many millions, contribute to education? Would that money, if invested in more academic or guidance efforts, make a difference by intense tutoring of the disadvantaged? The hall of fame suggests that money cannot overcome the obstacle of cultural attitudes. Athletics have an important place in an adolescent's life (I did a lot of that in my day but as outside-of-school activity). A school is for acquiring knowledge, which leads to equality of opportunity and hence to a better-balanced society.

Theodore Sizer, an experienced and very thoughtful educator, analyzes in *Horace's Compromise*[1] the multiple, intertwined, and conflicting difficulties facing high-school principals and teachers as they endeavor to provide quality education. Money (of which there's never enough), local politics, state mandates, union demands, and parental resistance combine to force compromises that result in lowered educational expectations. The typical American high school is thus the consequence of low expectations.

It's a national crisis, folks! A few are very aware of it; most Americans seem unperturbed. How long can we afford that?

What we need to do

We've examined what works well in our public education— all too little—and what doesn't—a whole lot. If easy solutions were possible, we would have implemented them by now. I propose steps below that will encounter hard cultural obstacles (though in America, we know, the impossible just takes a little longer). I also go into more detail in chapter 8, under "An education policy."

The evolution of a culture is delicate, and we cannot upset it by decree. Tampering with it can lead to unforeseen consequences. We need to let it pursue its natural pace over generations, but in education, we can steer it in the meantime in the desired direction. In fact, we already do. Much good, though not nearly enough, has happened in recent decades. All the positives I describe above under "the good" are barely half a century old and accelerating. We can do much if we muster the will and tease the culture. Immediate educational solutions lie within our society—in the community, in our government, and in how we value our teachers.

The community

In the American tradition, the community holds the main decision-making power in education. Today it has created a very few very good, breakthrough educational advances, notably charter and magnet schools, AP programs, and IBs.

The first public, community-sponsored charter school opened in 1974. In 2017, there were 6,900 of them, teaching 3.1 million students at all levels. Public (not private for-profit) charters maintain high quality. When they underperform, the state closes them. The first magnet school opened in 1968, and they, too, grew rapidly. In 1990, there were 232 of them, 1,400 in 2000 and 4,340 in 2020. They teach some 3.5 million students at all levels, and they, too, are held to high standards by their governing bodies.

These impressive numbers of students need clarification. The charter schools' numbers include elementary-school pupils, perhaps 30%. Also, not all charters are excellent. Some go sour and vanish—and their enrollments with them. As for magnets, some schools are entirely magnets, but others are regular high schools with a magnet option. In such cases, the number of magnet students represents a projected enrollment. It's a work in progress.

APs and IBs are new too. The first AP program began in 1955 with one modest class; the first IB programs opened in 1975. Both AP and IB are mainstays of charters and magnets and of our best traditional schools. All these great improvements are creations of engaged communities.

The Capitol Region Education Council (CREC) in central Connecticut offers a model of a broad community collaborating to provide educational excellence. The CREC has created an academic system that integrates all members of the community, overcoming economic and racial disparities. It began in 1966 and by the 1990s had evolved into a network of specialized magnet schools. Currently, it administers some seventeen of them at all levels. Seven are high schools, each attracting learners interested in particular academic tracks. One of them specializes in math and science, another in public safety, yet another in the arts. Still others in medical professions, in global and international studies, and iin environmental studies. The seventh, the Academy of Aerospace and Engineering, is the number-one high school in Connecticut and the thirteenth in the United States.

Collectively, these seven schools represent an alternative secondary-education model. They cater to a motivated student population that embarks on studies of presumed personal interest. They serve a full cross-section of their demographic catchment area: 30% White, 33% Black, and 28% Hispanic students; 47% disadvantaged. Of particular note, the best CREC schools register *no* proficiency gaps between White

and Black students. They employ motivated
teachers who teach subjects of personal
interest and competence, and they provide
these teachers with professional development.

Magnet schools tend to produce uncommon success in
the classroom. Of the thirty-three top American schools,
thirteen are magnets; a further six appear among the top
fifteen number-one state schools.

We must, of course, also credit communities for fostering a few excellent traditional high schools, like Walnut Hills
in Cincinnati. All such good schools—charters, magnets,
and traditional—express their communities' discontent with
educational mediocrity of low expectations, which indicates
that the community spirit in America is not on the wane, as
some fear. We may be bowling alone, but we care for our
young, though we may not always understand how to do it.

Indeed, the very scarcity of success examples like the
above points to the failure of the great majority of our communities to provide educational excellence. Most of our
schools neglect two aspects of the development of young
minds: organizing their thinking and teaching them to think
critically. If our communities systematically implemented
these two improvements *across the curriculum*, that alone
would move American education up from thirty-fourth.

Organizing thinking. The community also produces volunteerism, a trait ingrained in our culture. Volunteers tutor and
mentor high-school students and younger. My friend Mike
reports an experience that shows how our education can

improve through direct citizen involvement. He volunteered to mentor at a California high school, which designated him Silvana, a sophomore from a low-education home. At the beginning of the academic year, she was assigned an essay. She had no idea how to write it, didn't hand in a paper, and received a zero grade, which certainly didn't help her prospects. Mike began working with her when she was assigned a second essay and he watched her sitting, looking at the sheet of paper, unable to write a word. Mike realized that although she seemed smart, she had no idea how to organize thoughts. He taught her how to do that, and she wrote a successful essay.

The point is that Silvana wasn't taught how to organize what she knew, not at school, not at home. This fundamental deficiency probably afflicts millions. Covid-19 will probably cause lasting disruptions in the education of our young. The damage will likely harm most the children of the disadvantaged. As things stand with our high schools, the community will need a massive amount of that direct citizen involvement typified by Mike's mentoring (not always welcome by some teachers).

Thinking critically. The good schools, the volunteering, all these positive efforts are essential, of course, but we need also to mold citizens with analytical judgment. The kind who can differentiate rumors, lies, and conspiracy theories from facts based on data. Forming thinking citizens is emphatically the duty of education. Once one learns to organize one's thoughts, one is off to a better future. To become a better citizen, one needs to add critical and analytical thinking to organized thinking. Critical thinking approaches information open-mindedly, without preconception, questioning sources and searching for evidence. Teaching civics in that spirit must constitute an integral part of our schooling.

One would think that teaching to think critically is a universal good. I was partly educated by Jesuits. They taught us to question and hence to think. This turned out to be the most valuable consequence of all my years in schools, for the rest of my life. But in sections of our current society, thinking critically does not necessarily play well, especially when the community exerts sufficient adverse pressure. If an adolescent from a family that holds very traditional or religious values comes home and voices an opinion discovered in school from thinking critically, it may enrage the parent as heretical, sacrilegious, or worse. The parent confronts the principal, and there goes the teaching of critical thinking.

My friend Jerry deplores certain aspects of political correctness that create "trigger warnings" and "safe spaces"—taboo topics—lest exposure to such themes hurt some students' feelings. In some schools, the teaching of *The Odyssey* and *The Iliad* is taboo because slavery and rape may be involved. Taboos are the enemy of critical thinking. Adolescents protected from the controversial and the sensitive are prevented from learning about realities of life. During World War II, I attended a German school in German-occupied Yugoslavia. The school implicitly followed the Nazi ideology, and everything Jewish vanished from the curriculum—Jewish scientists, artists, authors, and composers no longer existed. This did not expand my knowledge or my ability to see diverse viewpoints (though Mendelssohn and Stefan Zweig dwelt at my home, quietly).

So, in that case, what do we do? We can vote for enlightened state superintendents of public instruction with the courage to stand up to the lobbies of ignorance and mandate the teaching of critical thinking as an integral part of the entire curriculum. While essential, that will not suffice to get us where our education should be. We need to think of more radical reforms.

The government

I propose a momentous reform. Across the land, some 26,000 school boards have failed to deliver an educational system that measures up to the demands of the modern world. We must think differently. The Founding Fathers contemplated only limited responsibilities for the federal government. These included foreign relations, defense, and, implicitly, domestic security. They did not include education. The present federal Department of Education (DOE) is a pale bureaucracy with mostly advisory functions. Today, that will not do. How educated our citizenry is, is as important as how well we equip our armed forces. Both deal with threats to our nation.

Congress must bring our education into the twenty-first century. It should mandate a reformed and greatly strengthened, appropriately funded, federal DOE. The reformed department would assume the primary role in formulating a national educational policy. It would establish and monitor national academic goals but also a strong vocational training system. The DOE would mandate specific standards for literacy, civics, and the STEM disciplines. It would also mandate the teaching of critical thinking throughout the curriculum at all levels in all public schools (that, of course, also affects the training of our teachers).

I advocate big government most reluctantly because I believe in the incalculable benefits of open thinking, experimentation, trial and error, and free contributions by all interested parties. It has worked to our great advantage in science, technology, and the economy, all benefiting from mostly well-judged government stimulation over recent decades. None of this happened in education. Time to stop doing what has proven not to work.

This reform will call for utmost thought and care, for fear of throwing out the baby with the bathwater. The educational successes I describe above under "the good" should remain in the hands of those who have created them and who manage them well now. The strengthened DOE would thus operate under a well-defined scope, leaving local school boards in charge of what they do effectively. The federal DOE would limit itself to establish and ensure reformed standards. Most importantly, it would assume a dominant role in the funding of public education.

That requires more fundamental rethinking. We spend more than any other country on education, and we get thirty-fourth for it. In 2016, we spent $13,600 per student on elementary and secondary education—39% higher than the average of the Organisation for Economic Co-operation and Development (OECD; a club of thirty-seven mostly rich countries), which stands at $9,800 per student.[11] The funding of our public education comes from the federal government, modestly, and from states' budgets and local taxes mostly. This varies greatly by state and locality. Meanwhile, excellence has come to depend on philanthropy. This results in profound disparities. Rube Goldberg could have designed it. Wealthy New Jersey ranks number one in college readiness (number two in reading, number two in math). It spends annually twenty thousand dollars per student. Poorer New Mexico ranks fiftieth in the nation (forty-ninth in reading, forty-ninth in math). It spends $9,600 per student. Some states may afford to spend more, but local ideologues may think little of the importance of education. Such disparities do nothing for our shared resilience. We need to consider the unthinkable—whether the federal government should assume the states' responsibility to fund public education. In chapter 8, under "A policy for education," I detail specifics.

But this is America, and we don't like anything imposed on us. The new curriculum cannot be rigid in structure and wooden in spirit. It needs to allow creative teachers to experiment within that framework, while helping the other teachers to clearly meet established goals. And it must attract and nourish student interest, not make the young feel that school is just a formal obligation. It is, first of all, about them.

The reformed DOE should be staffed by competent professionals, not by political appointees or by EdDs who have failed to prevent the present parlous state of our education.

And it must devote priority attention to those who teach. It should entirely reform our teacher education and recruitment system, because school boards, states, and schools of education have failed to do it. It must also create conditions for teacher unions to participate in and welcome change rather than resist it. A modern policy should result in carefully selected, well-paid, and respected teachers who will see their unions as professional associations rather than as industrial unions (see Finland below). The creation of rigorous admission exams for aspiring teachers, similar to the bar exam for lawyers, would enhance these objectives. Such exams would weed out marginal candidates and confer prestige on those admitted. A friend reports that in Houston (Texas), some teachers can't tell which is greater: $1/2$ or $1/3$. Such individuals would be prevented from contact with our young.

None of this will be easy. It will require taking the power of making often poorly considered scholastic decisions out of the hands of community school boards. It will need to overcome walls of deep-rooted mental habit. Our culture, especially in more conservative strongholds, doesn't see education in these terms.

Our teachers

No more "those who can, do; those who can't, teach." This abomination must disappear from our culture. One deleterious consequence of this antiquated state of mind is how we consider teachers, the most important and consequential of professions. We pay them badly because we don't respect them. To protect themselves from us, they form unions. What a scandal that those practicing the formation of future Americans, must protect themselves from the disdain of their fellow citizens!

I write these harsh words in sorrow. We have very many very competent and dedicated teachers who honor their profession. But they and their less-competent colleagues labor under excruciating conditions of a system set up not to provide quality education (see the box above about Theodore Sizer.)

The federal government must assume the responsibility to change our minds about our teachers' importance. It must make it a priority to provide conditions for the best among us to become teachers. Finland, admittedly very different from the United States, nevertheless offers an example.

The Center on International Educational Benchmarking reports that high-quality teachers are the hallmark of Finland's educational system. Theirs is "the most respected profession" and primary-school teaching the most sought-after career. Pay is not the motivator; it is reasonably competitive and comparable to that of other European countries. Their salaries, interestingly, mostly correspond to those of American teachers, though the economies are not comparable.

The teacher selection process itself confers prestige. Applicants must meet very high standards to be admitted to Finnish education programs. These programs, located at universities, not in teachers' colleges, accept only one in ten applicants, selecting from the top quartile of the applying

candidates. Teacher education forms an
integral part of universities, on par with
the most prestigious professions. Teachers
enjoy autonomy in how they apply Finland's
very ambitious and carefully thought-out
national curriculum. Hence, teaching has
many of the attractions of professions that
involve research, development, and design.
Finnish teachers engage annually in manda-
tory professional development. They belong
to unions, but these unions function in a
spirit of professional associations, not of
adversarial industrial unionism.

Is our public opinion ready for such a transformation?
Do we want our government to initiate it? We the People
must decide.

My faith in America comes, among other reasons,
from observing how some of our education has so greatly
improved over the past half century, spurred by community
and citizens' activist mobilization. Parents, teachers, concerned and philanthropic Americans, and businesses in their
self-interest have come together out of a sense of national
crisis. To bring change, they bypassed set-in-their-ways
school boards and teachers' unions that resisted reforms in
misconceived self-protection. In the next chapter on inventions and innovation, I report about the new educational initiatives resulting from new thinking and from technological

progress. They are too small so far but very promising. In such innovations we see, nonetheless, our culture evolving organically, stimulated by its natural instincts. The very essence of resilience. But it's not yet enough.

And a coda

Mark, a Russian boy, sixteen, recently moved to the United States from Russia, where he had received all his earlier education. He is smart and focused and has an appetite for knowledge. He now attends an American high school, where he takes AP courses. He is surprised by the difference between Russian and American systems. In Russian schools, he reports, memorizing sufficed. Here, he finds by contrast that new ideas and knowledge are discussed and digested rather than solely memorized (in an AP course). In Russia, he tells me, the curriculum is rigid through eleven years—no electives. In an American school, he is delighted that he can choose courses on subjects of interest to him and where different viewpoints are examined.

That is the best of our education, and we must retain it as a significant competitive advantage against our regimented adversaries Russia and China. In both communist and post-communist societies, discussions—that is, critical thinking—are discouraged or outright banned for obvious political reasons. Our open culture, at its best, educates our young to think; controlled societies, to memorize, not analyze.

Chapter 6

Inventiveness and Innovation

———◆———

As I began to plan this book, I had an intuition that Americans' inventiveness and their striving for change, improvement, and innovation had a direct connection to their society's resilience. As I decided to act on that intuition, I began to ask myself how invention and innovation can help us understand the march of our society over time. We can examine history conventionally by recording presidents, economic and social crises, and wars, civil or foreign. Or we can assess our history by following the effects of our national character. That path shows our destiny shaped by its restless appetite for material, intellectual, and moral change and improvement, destroying to create and innovate and, with that, to invent. I decided to follow that interpretation of America.

Indeed, inventiveness and innovation express the essence of American civilization's energy and creativity. The urge to invent was born with the country, in fact, even earlier. This essential trait of the national character has provided the engine that pulled our economy and our society through all its crises—the consistent mechanism of our resilience. Colonists already invented many useful and some scientific objects, none more than Benjamin Franklin. Their greatest invention, however, was not physical but intellectual: the creation of a new country on new principles of (relative) equality, freedom, and, implicitly, openness to change and innovation—a modern, revolutionary formulation of self-government.

In our inventions and the resulting innovations, we recognize ourselves—a young, restless nation, easily dismissing what is and replacing it with something better. Unlike older nations, comfortable in their traditional habits. Our inventiveness has remained vigorous, overcoming the vicissitudes of our history. Appendix 1 documents the incessant stream of financial calamities, mostly self-inflicted by our character, and the speed of their recoveries.

The telegraph, the telephone, the light bulb, and the assembly line originated amid financial crises. In fact, inventions and innovations provided the employment boosts, helping the country return to its normal growth and prosperity. For example, the 1885–88 recession saw a decrease of 14.6% in business activity, a deep economic crisis. Innovations came to the rescue: new electric street railways, employment growth in the inventive, young steel industry, advanced communications through the telephone, expansions in lighting,

the first cars that fueled the nascent oil market. All continued to propel the US economy, mitigating the effects of
recession—a token of resilience stemming from invention
and innovation.

The inventiveness itch is all-American and pertains
to our entire culture—to men and to women. We credit
famous men with famous inventions. But American women,
too, have produced a wealth of inventions. Some examples
among many more:

Table 6.1
Inventions by American Women

What	Who	When
Circular saw	Tabitha Babbitt	1813
Solar heating system	Mária Telkes	1948
Dishwasher	Josephine Graham	1886
Modern life raft	Maria Beasley	1882
Medical syringe	Letitia Geer	1899
Central heating	Alice Parker	1919
Electric refrigerator	Florence Parpart	1914
Caller ID and call waiting	Shirley Jackson	1970s
Kevlar fiber	Stephanie Kwolek	1969
Feeding tube	Bessie Blount Griffin	1948
Submarine lamp and telescope	Sarah Mather	1845
Laser cataract surgery	Patricia Bath	1988
Stem cell isolation	Ann Tsukamoto	1001

Incessant and all-encompassing, the native zest for innovation implies confidence and optimism.

Our inventions have transformed the world and have

shaped America's identity, none more than our Constitution. Invention/innovation benefit our prosperity, but they can cause transitions with painful consequences for individuals. Today we need to understand invention's and innovation's place in the wake of the four shocks described in chapter 1.

How invention leads to resilience

Let's take an example. The young republic at the beginning of the nineteenth century felt threatened by the European wars but had no weapons. In particular, it lacked muskets, which then were made individually by skilled craftsmen. It was slow, expert work, well remunerated, but it couldn't satisfy the numbers required by the small US Army. The government issued a contract to Eli Whitney, the inventor of cotton gin, for ten thousand muskets. He delivered, though tardily. The significance of how he did it is major. He invented the assembly line of prefabricated interchangeable parts. All his muskets were identical; all handmade muskets were different. Gunsmiths became obsolete.

Whitney's assembly line became known universally as the American System and created vast innovation in the United States and other industrialized nations. It now employed large numbers of semiskilled laborers, creating much unprecedented employment. The new factories assembled shoes, clocks, sewing machines, and many other products but put out of work skilled craftsmen and specialized mechanics. This process grew and prospered despite multiple economic crises in the nineteenth century.[1] The rapid increase of modern manufacturing helped resolve recessions more quickly because successive inventions produced innovations that led to renewed prosperity. Each new, employment-producing invention expressed our society's resilience by bolstering optimism and confidence.

During the golden age of American invention, spanning the nineteenth and early decades of the twentieth centuries, the major inventors were extraordinary individuals whose inventions smoothed economic cycles and reduced unemployment. Even lesser inventions helped abbreviate the unending economic crises. In 1828, Isaac Adams invented the power press, a great improvement in the printing of books, which now became easier and cheaper, greatly increasing the book market. Samuel Morse's telegraph created unprecedented sources of work: cable manufacturers, layers of cables and telegraph poles, and telegraph operators. It also reinvigorated newspapers; telegrams tied the nation together. Bell's telephone provided a similar shot into the economy's arm, followed by the massive advent of electricity from inventions of Edison and Tesla. From the 1880s through the 1920s, electricity-based inventions stimulated the economy: the light bulb, electric tramways, the gramophone, the cinema, the vacuum cleaner, the radio, the electric refrigerator, and countless more.

Henry Ford's continuously moving assembly line brought another revolutionary stimulus, and the 1920s saw not only millions of cars sold, but thousands of road miles paved, gas stations built, and car dealerships opened. All the while, the economy wobbled from recession to recession (see appendix 1), each promptly corrected by the stream of innovations. Once each invention became commercialized, it infused new employment in a branch of the economy that had not existed before. Inventiveness and innovation by individuals culminated in the 1920s. It all led to great prosperity and reckless exuberance and landed with a thud in October 1929, presenting a new challenge to America's resilience.

Beginning in the eighteenth century and essentially into the 1920s, American inventions sprouted from individuals. The grand exception was the US Constitution, a collective product. Very few of the great inventions of that period benefited from government funding. Following World War II, important inventions resulted more often from collective enterprise and became funded by the government or by corporations.

Breakthroughs now demanded increasing sophistication, which required teamwork between those possessing advanced technical skills and those with state-of-the-art scientific knowledge. The experimentations of a single inventor, no matter how brilliant, no longer sufficed in many cases. From team efforts came the atomic bomb (regrettably, wars have stimulated many consequential inventions), the polio vaccine (Jonas Salk received government grants and gathered a team of researchers), the vast array of scientific and technical advances that allowed the moon walk of 1969, the internet and its infinite trail of inventions, MRI, a torrent of medical discoveries, artificial intelligence, the human genome map, and gene replacement, among others.

Some brilliant individuals continued nevertheless in the American tradition of personal initiative. Such was prolific Steve Jobs, who invented the Apple Macintosh computer, the iPhone, and the iPad, among others (aided, of course, by teams of specialists). Exceptional individual inventors now encountered a much more sophisticated, multidisciplinary universe of knowledge.

In the 1970s, venture capitalists began to materialize. Their money and judgment for talent have given a massive boost to American innovation. California's Silicon Valley is the most famed of their successes (Google, Apple, Tesla, Facebook, and myriad others), but their influence has grown nationwide. Venture capital clusters mostly around major universities that produce inventive minds. Thus, in Seattle around the University of Washington, in San Diego around University of California campuses, in Nashville around Vanderbilt University, in North Carolina's Research Triangle around three large and influential universities, and, of course, around Boston and other distinguished academic sites in the nation. Venture capitalists fund individuals and spawn teams.

This accumulation of American creations over more than two centuries has contributed mightily to modernizing the world. Of course, not all inventions had history-changing consequences. Nonetheless, the humble paper clip and many thousands of other American inventions, big and small, have made everyday life better across the planet.

So how are we doing?

Does our inventiveness remain vigorous still? Some doubt it. They juxtapose the golden age of individual inventors with the recent sixty or so years, during which most inventions stemmed from teams of researchers funded by government and corporations. In this, the skeptics see a retreat of the bounty of our inventiveness. Are they right? Perhaps, but the cornucopia of applications for the smartphone suggests that the independent inventor is still with us. In 2015, the US Patent Office granted 24,365 patents to independent inventors, many of them smartphone application developers.

Still, the skeptics' concerns deserve consideration because inventiveness is intimately related to resilience. Inventiveness rises in a climate of optimism and confidence and declines with uncertainty. Patent applications over time illustrate these fluxes. Table 6.2 with data from the US Patent Office demonstrates fluctuations of patent applications over 170 years (the numbers are rounded up).[2]

Table 6.2

Decade	Average yearly # of patent applications	US population (millions)
1851–1860	4,000	31.4
1861–1870	12,000	38.5
1871–1880	21,000	51.2
1881–1890	34,000	63.0
1891–1900	39,000	76.2
1901–1910	55,000	92.2
1911–1920	69,000	106.9
1921–1930	84,000	123.2
1931–1940	63,000	142.6
1941–1950	62,000	161.3
1951–1960	74,000	189.3
1961–1970	99,000	212.3
1971–1980	105,000	236.5
1981–1990	127,000	158.7
1991–2000	216,000	291.4
2001–2010	405,000	308.7
2011–2019	579,000	328.7

Several observations stand out.

The 1860s show a considerable leap from the turbulent 1850s that led to the Civil War. In fact, most of the growth of patent applications in the 1860s followed the Civil War. Little invention occurred in the first half of the decade. In the peace years after 1865, the applications tripled.

During the last three decades of the nineteenth century, a period of great inventions but also of great financial instability and economic uncertainty, the numbers of applications seem proportionately modest.

Patent applications rise abruptly during the first decade of the twentieth century, a period of economic growth and prosperity.

They decline through the Great Depression and World War II uncertainties but take off during the Cold War, another period largely of peace and prosperity. Military inventions, the internet among them, and the fast growth of uses of the computer predominate.

Patent applications gallop into the twenty-first century. However, now the US Patent Office grants many patents to foreign companies and so numbers no longer solely reflect American inventiveness. Of the 579,000 applications from the entire world in the latest decade, 25% were American, amounting to a healthy 145,000 applications.

What to conclude? The uninterrupted growth of American patent applications attests to a steady, resilient continuity through times good and bad. We need to look at these data more closely, however. Despite being relatively few, the patent applications during the Golden Age produced major discoveries. Now we produce hundreds of thousands of patent applications yearly. Are they of transcendental significance still? Many are trivial (Post-it Notes, microwave popcorn bags), but others continue to affect how the entire world operates. In the last fifty years, we find among them the following American inventions:

Table 6.3

The lunar module and all attendant science and technology	The internet with all its consequences (email, Facebook, YouTube, etc.)
Hubble Space Telescope	Smartphone
Personal computer	Stealth bomber
Laser printer	Email
Human genome map	Civil and military drones
Space shuttle	Google search
Antilock brakes	Bioartificial liver
MRI	3-D ocean farms
3-D printing	Digital camera
anti-cholesterol drugs	

Impressive, certainly. All that and more influences the universe beyond our borders. But we need to note that the US Patent Office in 2019 granted 186,188 patents to US applicants but 201,986 to those from the rest of the world. That is in addition to the millions of national patents granted by other countries. Some foreign patents may only be knockoffs of

American inventions. These numbers still deserve our attention, even if we may produce more important breakthroughs than the rest. We can interpret the entire world coveting American patents as universal confidence in our continuity. But we should be aware of the threat of complacency.

The *Harvard Business Review* (May 27, 2014), under the title "Why Germany Dominates the U.S. in Invention," discusses the great strides Germans are making in invention. The article makes a valid, though exaggerated, claim of German superiority. The excellence of German cars does not carry the same impact as, say, the internet. And even when it comes to cars, American Tesla stands in a new category from all preceding. The car itself and the entire concept of its production and marketing bespeak radical innovation and not merely technical German excellence in traditional products.

So now we compete, but with rare exceptions, we appear to no more than hold our own. Yet we used to dominate in inventiveness! So perhaps the doubters are right and we don't invent as much as we used to (taking into account the quadrupling of our population since the nineteenth century). Is the rest of the world catching up, or are we relatively slowing down? If we are, we need to examine what may hinder the growth of our inventiveness.

Addressing headwinds

How will our propensity to invent respond to the shocks described in chapter 1? It faces four headwinds: our attitude

toward science, our views on immigration, our hesitant will-
ingness to accept change, and the displacement, training and
retraining of our work force.

Science

From the later years of the nineteenth century, American
inventions began to depend on science, as for Nikola Tesla
and Alexander Graham Bell. In those years, the German
research university concept reached America. Johns Hopkins
University in Baltimore was founded in 1876, expressly as
a research university. It modeled itself after then-promi-
nent Heidelberg University (where, incidentally, my Russian
grandfather had studied in the 1880s). Science in America
quickly took off. Other universities followed Johns Hopkins
in rapid succession. The 1893 World's Columbian Exposition
in Chicago signaled the arrival of science at the popular level.
The exhibition was completely electrified in the first massive
use of electricity in the United States, and Nikola Tesla conducted public scientific experiments at the exhibition.

Promptly, America became a hotbed for the sciences.
Increasingly through the twentieth century, science prospered and proliferated in the United States. We now had
first-rate universities, among the best in the world, producing sophisticated research, and our researchers investigated
in the world's finest laboratories. Some of the top scientists
from other countries gravitated to America, where they
found a cultural climate most favorable to thinking freely
and where they could benefit from liberal funding. They
could also work with first-rate professional colleagues. The

results in table 6.3 above speak for themselves. The atomic bomb was a truly international, though regrettable, scientific and technical effort on US soil.

So what's to worry about science? Well, it turns out, plenty. Hostility for one, supply for another.

Hostility

Large segments of our population lack any scientific knowledge. A detailed report of the Pew Research Center on Science and Society concludes that in 2019, only about six out of ten Americans possessed considerable knowledge or an awareness of science.[3] This leaves millions who do not (recent surveys show that 28% of Americans don't know that the earth rotates around the sun, and 555% can't define DNA). While not necessarily hostile to science, such citizens remain open to an atmosphere of actively undermining trust in science that festers in our country in the early twenty-first century.[4]

In this climate, especially during the 2017–2021 Trump administration, religious organizations and social media have contributed variously to science hostility. Political calculations caused that administration to systematically undermine confidence in science. It contradicted scientific medical information in fighting covid-19, it denied that the climate is changing, and it weakened environmental protection. A significant segment of religious opinion— the Christian right—finds science generally objectionable, apparently because it contradicts the literal interpretation of the Bible. In opposing the teaching of evolution, such groups conduct a mini-crusade against science. A considerable segment of opinion, fanned by social media rumors, opposes vaccination. They offer various reasons, religious, sanitary, political, and mythical.

Hostility toward or suspicion of science has severely damaging consequences. Medically, it hampers combatting effectively infectious diseases and making fundamental scientific discoveries. Scientific ignorance leads to the abuse of antibiotics, thereby reducing their effectiveness. Politically, it separates us into populations that don't share a common understanding of the modern world—another impediment to national resilience. Worst, educationally, it prevents modern knowledge from developing the minds of our young.

Supply

Most modern inventions require, as we saw, scientific researchers. Our universities produce modest numbers of PhDs awarded to US citizens and residents in the sciences, mathematics, and statistics (in 2018, 256 in the sciences and 1,960 in mathematics and statistics).[5] The great majority opt for academic teaching careers, not for cutting-edge basic research. That kind of research is conducted at a few leading national and private research labs and at leading universities. Industry-based applied research, including healthcare, pays very well but demands high competence, a great deal of effort, and important results. Academia-based scientific research, say at the Massachusetts Institute of Technology (MIT), the Ivy League, the top campuses of the University of California, and a couple of dozen other world-leading American universities, employs the finest researchers. For these individuals, generous funding comes from the government and foundations. They create the innovations that drive our society. But those few top-notch scientists dwell in a rarefied world. We need to expand that world greatly. For basic and applied research to thrive, we must cause our government to invest large funds in research of all kinds. It's what allowed us to walk on the moon. I expand on this in chapter 8 under "Priority legislation."

Here, concerns about supply come in. As we saw in chapter 5 on education, PISA data place our high schoolers twenty-eighth in the world in science and thirty-sixth in mathematics (no science without math). Which hints at an unpromising future. Not coincidentally, foreign-born US residents had created 35% of all American innovations as of February 2016.[6] Which leads us into:

Immigration again

Nikola Tesla, a Serb, and Alexander Graham Bell, a Scot, created transcendental scientific innovations. Thousands of inventions by other immigrants followed them, some major, some minor. Among the consequential, Swedish engineer David Lindquist, while working for the Otis Elevator Company, produced a series of patented inventions that led to the creation of the electric elevator in the 1920s. Another was German chemist Hermann Frasch, a contemporary of Bell and Tesla, a prolific inventor with sixty-four US patents. His most notable inventions led to the current processes of fracking oil.

Among minor immigrant inventions, we find the hamburger, the doughnut, and blue jeans. Both the grand and the small influence the world beyond our borders. As I travel to my native and often reflexively anti-American France, I am shocked to find the natives wolfing down hamburgers (1.4 billion of them in 2018) while also wearing blue jeans. Simple, immigrant-created inventions that express the casual informality of American culture and seduce the world, even in the home of the cuisine.

Nobel Prizes tell another story about the value of creative immigrants. In twenty years, between 2000 and 2020, fifteen American immigrants received Nobels in physics, 43% of all American Nobels in that science. In chemistry, immigrants received twelve Nobels, 35% of all American Nobels in that category. And in medicine, immigrants received ten Nobels, 32% of all American Nobels in that field.[7] This is how that looks in a table:

Table 6.4

Category	Immigrant	Native-Born	Percentage of Immigrants Winners
Physics	15	20	43%
Chemistry	12	22	35%
Medicine	10	21	32%
Total	37	63	37%

Since 1960, immigrants received some 35% of all American Nobels in the sciences. Yet in chapter 4 on immigration, we saw that large numbers of American natives oppose all immigration, seeing no difference between illegal and legal. Fadel Adib, a young Lebanese, completed a bachelor's degree with highest honors at the American University in Beirut and then a master's and a PhD at MIT. He stayed, now an immigrant, and is an associate professor of computer science at MIT. He leads a team in investigating subsea sensor technologies.

We don't want thinking immigrants? How very stupid!

Addressing accelerating change

At first glance, our eager readiness to accept change seems in rude health. Just about everybody owns a smart-phone or similar device with all the pertinent applications. Such change is easy to adopt because it enriches one's expe-riences and costs little more than a few hundred dollars. When change disrupts or harms our lives, it becomes less easy to accept.

From K–12 and into colleges and universities, technolog-ical innovations, mostly American, have invaded education over the past two decades.[8] Their acceptance and implemen-tation have risen rapidly, given an extra spur by covid-19. Technological advances have led to teaching and learning innovations: personalized learning, blended learning, one-on-one computing, massive open online courses (MOOC), and online testing, among others. These changes in our edu-cational system are irreversible because enough have already proven beneficial. In 2011, two Stanford professors offered the university's first MOOC (free). They were astounded when 160,000 students from 190 countries enrolled. What astounded in 2011 has evolved into a variety of online educa-tional innovations, not free anymore because MOOCs gener-ated marketable ideas. In 2019, the market value of the new educational technology was worth some forty-three billion dollars and is growing rapidly.

This new industry is still a work in progress as users search for optimal applications. Not all works well—some technical problems need resolving; some privacy concerns have arisen. That novelty causes discomfort and controversy. Teachers need to adapt, and so do parents and learners. For some, these changes are wrenching. Good teachers, with decades of successful experience, need to learn novel methods and thinking. They can feel imposed upon. But these changes cause no social damage such as loss of jobs or displacement of faculty. On the whole, these innovations, while uncomfortable to some during a transition period, benefit society by giving a new impulse to education and thus enhancing our resilience.

Not all vast changes can enhance our society's resilience. A cascade of critical inventions in automation of business and government processes, robotization of manufacturing, and conversion of traditional retailing to online commerce have carved deep employment fissures in our society. Such creative destruction, historically American, probably never reached the current rate and scale, not even during the transition from agriculture to factory work. Does change through accelerating invention and innovation now undermine our resilience by affecting some more than others?

I described above how Eli Whitney created the assembly line of interchangeable parts and how that invention had profound consequence on employment. Many skilled craftsmen became obsolete, and much larger numbers of the semiskilled found jobs. Whitney's invention and other great ones boosted the prosperity of the country, but they also came at a great personal cost to many. That pattern repeated itself throughout American history, hugely so today.

The McKinsey Global Institute report of November 28, 2017, projects that as much as one-third of the US labor force may be replaced by automation, including robots, by 2030. To this automation scenario, we need to add the effects of online marketing. CNBC reported on April 14, 2020, that 7.5 million small businesses were at risk of closing permanently as a consequence of online marketing, a trend accelerated by covid-19.[9] Not to mention major store chains. *Forbes* reported on May 30, 2020, "Macy's Will Furlough the Majority of Its 125,000 Employees."

These estimated numbers may eventually vary in detail, but their immensity presents an unprecedented challenge to our resilience. Unlike preceding reasons for unemployment caused by economic miscalculation or financial speculation and skullduggery, these numbers result from our inventions, from deliberate destruction to create new and better. If we can seamlessly absorb those disrupted and unemployed, we can see the nation still inventive and prone to change. So let's consider displacement of our labor.

Worker displacement, training, and retraining

The above McKinsey report also projects the creation of many new jobs in a great variety of economic activities. Statista (December 11, 2019) reported that in 2019, there were 774,725 new small businesses, less than a year old, employing some 1.8 million. Should such numbers persist and should the economy not wobble through the 2020s, new businesses should potentially reabsorb many of those displaced by automation and online commerce. Major existing businesses should also help. For example, in 2020, Amazon employed 850,000. In the same vein, the US Census reports that during the covid-19 year of 2020, 550,000 new business applications were received—an 83% increase over the previous record.

But for innovation to thrive, we must resolve a major obstacle. Most new jobs will require more knowledge, new skills, and hence more education or training. In addition to various degrees of competence in the latest technology and science, new jobs will demand higher levels of mastery of mathematics and especially of analytical thinking to make sense of an ocean of data. Unless quickly retrained, those displaced will join the ranks of the unemployed on an enormous scale. Can we do it?

The issues to confront include not only displacements but also replacements. Many retirements over the next decade will help. A younger, better-educated, and trained cohort will take their places. As for displacements, if indeed we must find more sophisticated employment for 30% of the workforce, we need to contemplate a national effort of possibly unprecedented extent, perhaps comparable to the mobilizations of the Second World War. We must not lose sight of the increasingly more sophisticated requirements of our economy.

Some tools already exist in our education system or are under construction—themselves recent results of American inventiveness and innovation. They go under the general label of work-based learning. Currently located mostly in high schools, they combine rigorous academic instruction with work-applicable skills and offer internships at potential employers. This movement grows simultaneously in several forms and at various sites. Among these initiatives, we find:

- *P-TECH*. A program sponsored initially by IBM but at this writing, it is now supported by hundreds of other businesses. It operates at regular public high schools, lasts six years, and offers a high school diploma and an associate's degree in a specific field. In 2019, over one hundred schools offered it, and many more are adopting it. P-TECH favors the STEM (science, technology, engineering, mathematics) disciplines. Graduates are not obligated to take jobs at IBM, though some do.

- *National Academy Foundation (NAF)*. It operates "academies" in regular high schools and offers programs to prepare students for the workplace. Its curricula include particular preparation in finance, hospitality and tourism, information technology, engineering, and health sciences. In 2018, NAF academies functioned at 620 schools, with 122,000 students. Its programs produce very successful results and benefit from the support of major corporations like Verizon, Marriott, Raytheon, Optum, AT&T, United Technologies, Hewlett-Packard, Oracle, and others.

- *Linked Learning*. This online education business offers access to some sixteen thousand expert-led courses that help with preparation for the world of work and allow learners to earn course-completion certificates.

- *Cengage*. A large college textbook publisher, it listed 480 work-applicable online courses on its website in 2021.

Cengage is expanding its online business, responding to an emerging need that conventional academic courses and textbooks cannot address.

These and similar programs, though still new and small but already successful and promising, provide a template that we can expand to massively retrain our workforce. To achieve the necessary expansion, a vast mobilization of pertinent contributors must occur. As I argue in chapter 5 on education, the federal government must provide organization and significant funding. (In 2021, the Biden administration planned such programs specifically for Black-owned small businesses.) Business, in its self-interest, must become committed. IBM with P-TECH shows the way. If thus fired up, these educational forces can go a long way to retrain our workforce for the coming challenge but not before the teaching profession buys in. Teachers, underappreciated and underpaid, will have to provide the indispensable fulcrum to get this retraining underway. Their unions are notoriously suspicious of change and reforms lest they damage the gains already obtained by their members. The federal government must step in to provide incentives for the teaching profession. That is a national priority.

Innovation cuts both ways. It can cause immense displacements. It can create the solutions.

The United States competes with the world. Our inventiveness has always given us the edge because it produced major breakthroughs, time after time. China, for instance,

produces myriads of patents. They don't represent concep-
tual breakthroughs but rather refinement of existing knowledge, some of which is likely purloined from us. They didn't
invent the assembly line, the telegraph, the telephone, the
light bulb, MRI, the major medical breakthroughs of the
twentieth century, the science that took us to the moon, the
internet, or the iPhone. Or pioneered flight, as the Wright
brothers did. All of these American inventions and innovations came to dominate the world.

We need to continue inventing, including achieving con-
ceptual breakthroughs and not only refinements of existing
inventions. We need to invest abundantly in research and
development (R&D) as a national strategy. The government
(that is, all of us) needs to promote R&D on a national scale
and fund it at the leading universities and research labs
to prove us resilient again in the wake of covid-19 and the
displacements caused by our innovations. Our abundant
inventiveness worked amid crises in the second half of the
nineteenth century. We can do it.

Chapter 7

The Economy
in Novel Times

———— ◆ ————

The economy provides another measure of our resilience. It can be prosperous and infuse confidence and optimism. Or it can be the opposite.

Despite all the talk about China, America's economy remains by far the strongest in the world and is likely to continue so over the immediate future, propelled by our technological and scientific prowess and by optimistic entrepreneurial and investor behavior. This strength will not benefit all Americans equally. In February 2020, our unemployment stood at a low of 3.5%. Post-covid-19, this low rate will not soon return. In preceding chapters, I previewed reasons for our economic disruptions: disparities in education, potentially very large unemployment from automation and e-commerce, small business destructions by covid-19, and an inadequate supply of highly educated brains who can produce innovation. These disruptions will probably persist in varying degrees over the next decade, bringing uncertainties to individuals, even if some measures of the broad economy, such as the stock market, continue to perform favorably.

New norms will rule that economy. Covid-19 has affected countless lives and pocketbooks. Some sectors will undergo radical changes or will even disappear. For those employed in the travel and hospitality industries, the recovery should stabilize fairly promptly. Not so for retail commerce. In turbulent 2020, various estimates projected permanent closures of a broad range of businesses, from hundreds of thousands to 7.5 million. Whatever the actual figures, individual consequences for many will hit hard. Entirely new patterns of employment will appear that will depend on improved education, replacing millions of jobs lost during covid-19 and from the transition to a rapidly automating economy. New work and commute habits will require personal adaptations. The federal government has injected massive subsidies into the ailing economy. How much is enough before these subsidies weaken some initiative and risk-taking desire?

How we respond to these changes will define our resilience. To gain an understanding, we need to consider four major influences affecting our economy through the decade of the 2020s:

- Radical effects of progress in *technology*

- *Employment* patterns resulting from technological change

- *Commerce* patterns resulting from technological change

- The powerful links between the economy
  and *public health*

Technology's influence

The computer in its many manifestations—the internet, automation, information technology, machine learning and artificial intelligence, e-commerce, social media, data analysis—governs our economic future. We should expect technology to bring great benefits but also great disruptions to our existences.

In 1996, times prehistoric in computer technology, I cofounded CyberGnostics, an online educational publishing company, in partnership with Jessica Utts, professor of statistics at the University of California, Davis. Theretofore, I published college textbooks in the usual print-on-paper form. CyberGnostics published exclusively online. No paper, though students could print out our materials. Books required students to learn through imagination and memorization.

Thanks to the internet, our system allowed
them to do the unprecedented: to learn by
manipulating ideas and data on the screen
and not solely by reading. They could now
experiment with abstract concepts by visual-
izing their entire unfolding, change variables
to understand them fully, and thus achieve
what a few static graphics in a book couldn't.

CyberGnostics taught us some modern
ideas. First, that the internet made the
unimaginable quite effortless and pedagog-
ically beneficial. Secondly, that it was easy
and cheap to start a modest enterprise. Our
company's world headquarters was my desk
at home. No office to rent and no file cabinets
to buy. It was all in the cloud. We had no
payroll. Our staff consisted of contractors,
spread around the country and instantly
contactable. Same for our authors, whom we
paid royalties on sales. We didn't generate
any employment, just some extra income to
the gig sector. Our effect on the economy
was, of course, imperceptible. The third
lesson was that new ideas are accepted by
the mentally alert and resisted by the rest.
Of course, interactive learning online has
grown colossally since our modest effort.
Millions around the world use it now.

The good

This story illustrates the hardly imaginable just a few decades ago. Computer technologies have brought unimaginable changes and improvements. Gigantic gains in time savings, in cost reductions, in fact, in so many services available for free.

This allows drastic cost reductions in all phases of the economy—in manufacturing and in the provision of services, ranging from law to radiology. E-commerce saves driving, parking, time, and money while quickly delivering access to unlimited choices. Smartphones deliver infinite and mostly free access to sources of information, to the important and the trivial. They have also created social media with all its effects, not always desirable. Video conferencing saves costs in time and money, substituting for travel. For some, car or even plane travel may become superfluous. Distance learning holds vast potential to make education more effective, as I discuss in earlier chapters and in the above example. Some will greatly benefit, but those not integrated into the computer universe will not.

The uncertain

Technology will force great changes on how we conduct business. The economy will need to respond to new consumer behaviors and expectations. Commerce, national and international, will change significantly, and much of it will move online. Many brick-and-mortar businesses will close, and small businesses will struggle to survive. Automation will affect livelihoods in rural communities and small towns differently than in large urban centers—manufacturing mostly in the former, services mostly in the latter. This will further emphasize differences between metropolitan and small-er-town America. As the internet's influence grows, it will upend one economic activity after another: manufacturing, newspapers, bookstores. Entire industries have disappeared (Blockbuster, Bethlehem Steel). Entirely new activities have arisen (Amazon.com, Netflix, PayPal, Zoom). Semi-monopolistic giants like Google, Microsoft, or Facebook may expand their dominances. Cryptocurrencies and self-driv-ing cars create new quandaries.

> The demise of Blockbuster, a rental business of movies on DVD, exemplifies an inability to anticipate and understand the advent and stunning rapidity of technological change. The company was founded in Texas in 1985 and prospered mightily for two decades. At its peak in the early 2000s, it had nine thousand stores worldwide. In 1997, Reed Hastings, a customer disgruntled by what he considered high-handed Blockbuster policies, conceived and founded Netflix. It provided the same films online, cheaper and much more conveniently. Blockbuster man-agement, blinded by success, failed to under-stand this competition and dismissed the possibility of buying Netflix in its infancy. In 2010, Blockbuster declared bankruptcy. Its sixty thousand workers (worldwide) lost their jobs. At this writing, Netflix employs 7,100.

If, over the next decade, we manage competently and wisely this technologic transition of gains in new jobs and losses in existing ones, we should be able to balance gains and losses. Maintaining our confidence and optimism will depend on our ability to perform this transition.

Employment patterns

As more activities become automated or robotized, employment will change, to the benefit of some and to the detriment of others. Computerization has already created a profound income gap between those engaged in it and those outside. The Pew Research Center (May 7, 2019) evaluated this "digital divide" and reported that those earning less than thirty thousand dollars (29% of the working population) showed a low adoption of computer technology, whereas those earning above $100,000 had adopted computer technology to a high degree.[1] In this sense, the economy extends another distancing between Americans.[2]

In the 2020s, employment prospects will thus not favor those who fail to adapt to change. The service sector, which employs four out of five Americans, will require particular attention. It includes janitors and surgeons, bankers and professors, lawyers and trainers, security guards and retail clerks, accountants and stock brokers, and myriad other occupations. Automation threatens all of them in various degrees.

Professionals in the STEM fields will do well. They include a great variety of researchers, including computer scientists, artificial intelligence and software developers, security specialists, and similar information technology specialists. They come equipped with (more often advanced) higher education, and their employment prospects appear firm. Good for our resilience.

High-tech industries show solid growth prospects. Microsoft, Google, Facebook, Amazon, and Apple ride the rising surf of computerization and should continue to employ large numbers. At this writing, Amazon, the most labor-intensive, employs some 950,000, ranging from warehouse workers to computer scientists. Though each of the other four employs fewer—Facebook some 45,000, Microsoft some 160,000, Apple some 147,000, and Google some 121,000—the significance of these numbers resides in their multiplier effect. Economists calculate that for every new full-time high-tech hire, the multiplier effect results in an additional 4.3 jobs created, largely in the economy's service sector.[3] So every new high-tech hire effectively creates 5.3 jobs. This effect applies to actual hires and doesn't when jobs are replaced by gig contractors. Potentially good for resilience.

The health-based sector—medicine, pharmacology, instrumentation, hospitals, and scientific research—is a huge employer. In 2018, some sixteen million persons worked in medicine alone (doctors, related professionals, nurses, support personnel), plus well over 300,000 in pharmacology and hundreds of thousands more in various health-related fields. The covid-19 crisis has already spurred much preparation, planning, and innovation in public health in anticipation of further epidemics. Pharmacologic manufacture may also grow because relying on a manufacturing monopoly of many critical drugs in China has proven risky. Automation will cut some jobs, but overall employment in healthcare professions will grow by 15% between 2019 and 2029, according to the US Bureau of Labor Statistics, spurred by, among other factors, the aging of our population. Good for resilience.

In manufacturing, automation and robotization will enhance its entire range of activities. In employment, the computer will cut both ways. It will eliminate jobs and create others.[4] By replacing human workers, manufacturing automation makes for reliably higher product quality and consistency while also providing a safer workplace. Robotic automation will paradoxically create many new, well-paying jobs across the economy: in engineering, systems analysis and design, and data analysis; in control of manufacturing itself; and in systems integration. Of course, these will be sophisticated jobs, not replacing workers displaced by lack of training. Probably unfavorable for resilience.

New manufacturing forms will create new employment. A great amount of work goes into reconceiving and enhancing batteries, into 3-D printing, into electric and self-driving vehicles. Initial employment will be modest (the battery industry employed forty-five thousand in 2019), but these new industries promise fast growth. Some older manufacturing will lose employees. Boeing, for example, is intensely automating the building of its airplanes and will shed workers. Probably neutral to slightly positive for resilience.

Government employment, which in 2020 represented 20% of total jobs, will probably remain steady or slightly grow at all levels as its unions will fight automation. The government-funded public sector will probably see increased employment because of investments in infrastructure, at least as long as Democrats govern the federal administration. On the whole, neutral on resilience.

A broad range of white-collar professions and occupations in the service sector will have different prospects. Financial industries, including banking, insurance, and various forms of investment firms, will see reductions at the lower clerical levels, susceptible to automation. For most professions, demand for the well-educated should cause steady and even growing employment. At lower levels, much automation has already taken place, and it will continue. Again, in all these service sectors, the level of education will be decisive. On the whole, probably unfavorable for resilience.

Creative types—artists, actors, writers, painters, musicians—cannot be automated. The likely overall prosperity of our society should increase demand for them, including in advertising, promotion, and decoration. Favorable for resilience.

The retail sector will exact a heavy toll on employment. A combination of a rapid rise of e-commerce and of consequences of covid-19 causes a debacle in the physical plant part of this sector. Its replacement, the virtual sector, e-commerce, will employ proportionately fewer. Projections of retail employment losses vary, but all agree that online retail firms operate efficiently with fewer workers. Giants of retail are failing or struggle on life support; massive numbers of small businesses are closing for not-so-good. Not good for resilience.

Which takes us to the very important topic of independent

(gig) work. Over 36% of working Americans participated in it in 2019, and 43% are projected to elect this kind of work by 2023.[5] Large numbers of the newly unemployed may aspire to become self-employed contract workers. But gig work requires specialized competencies—college instructors, book editors, and graphic designers come to mind—among infinite other skill-based occupations. Most require up-to-date education (occupations such as delivery drivers don't need specialized skills). How many of those losing their jobs in the changing economy can qualify for (or would want dubiously remunerated) gig work?[6] Again, unpromising for resilience.

A great number of technicians will also remain in demand and will need training beyond high school. They include traditional trades such as plumbers, who now require computer training, and new ones in certain health fields, in solar panel and wind turbine installation, and in a great variety of other technical medical activities. Some entirely new occupations will arise, as in this sampler (some already have): cyber city analyst, robot dispatcher, artificial intelligence assistant, data scientist, software engineer, security engineer, solutions architect, systems engineer, 3-D printing chemist, digital marketer, and solar panel installer, among countless novel others. If we are able to train them, good for resilience.

Which brings us back to education. Some of these jobs will require higher education, some will not, but none can be filled by someone holding a high-school diploma only. The education system will require drastic changes (beginning in earliest childhood), as I discuss in chapter 5 on education and chapter 6 on inventiveness and innovation. The

computerization of the entire range of our economy will
place more stringent educational requirements for employment. There is much room for pessimism among those little
educated.

Patterns of commerce

Commerce, a wealth creator crucial to economic vitality, will
undergo wrenching changes over the next decade. Much in
its physical conformation will change; social habits and traditions will fade, and some will disappear. This will have not
only economic consequences. Since earliest historic times,
in Mesopotamia or in Egypt, commerce was conducted
person to person. A buyer, perhaps a housewife, would stop
by a merchant's stall and make a purchase. Maybe there was
banter, maybe haggling, but there was personal contact.

> Some decades ago, my canny Yankee wife
> stopped in a store in Marrakech that sold
> paraphernalia of appeal to tourists. My
> wife showed interest in a tribal dagger.
> The merchant named a price, and my
> wife gave him a look like, "You are joking."
> Some bargaining took place. Then my wife
> thanked the merchant, and we walked out
> of the store. He came running after us
> and invited us to have mint tea. My wife, of
> course, expected that—part of the theater
> of commerce in a Middle Eastern culture

> (though we were in Morocco). We had
> pleasant tea and chatted, and gradually a
> price was agreed upon. We parted friends.
> That dagger now decorates my office.

For millennia, commerce was conducted in that spirit, though more soberly in efficient northern Europe. The American yen for innovation changed traditional ways in commerce too. In 1852, Harry Gordon Selfridge opened Marshall Field's in Chicago, the first modern department store. That created a second phase of commerce, where the merchant no longer interacted personally with customers, but the clerks did. Supermarkets and shopping malls followed. The personal relationship began to vanish, but customer convenience grew greatly.

We have now entered a third phase of commerce. It operates online and has erased personal interactions. Much as this new form of commerce may provide convenience; it has severed social bonds when they should be particularly valuable to a society politically, culturally, socially, and economically divided. One more aspect of America where we don't speak face to face. Personal isolation favors political polarization.

The transition to all-embracing e-commerce steams ahead unstoppable into uncharted territory, further stimulated by the effects of covid-19. The consequences for the economy are profound. In February 2020, Macy's announced that it will close 125 of its department stores by 20203. Nordstrom, too, is closing many stores, and J.Crew, Neiman Marcus, Brooks Brothers, Ann Taylor, and JCPenney declared bankruptcy in 2020. Bed Bath & Beyond teeters on the verge of it and closed two hundred stores that year. None of that stimulates resilience.

The National Bureau of Economic Research estimated in April 2020 that 100,000 small businesses will close permanently over the coming decade. Some because of the migration of their clientele to the online world. Others because of the catastrophic conditions imposed by the covid-19 pandemic. Among those, hospitality (hotels, restaurants, cafés) and the travel industry (airlines, cruise lines) because of covid-reduced travel. Barbers, beauticians, fitness studios, and countless others will follow. Commercial real estate (office buildings, stores, shopping malls) will undergo severe to fatal losses. Why rent offices when you can work from home? Why pay rent for a store when you can advertise services online and through social media? Essential plumbers and electricians or businesses catering to more expensive tastes will not suffer. And gratifying to me as a publisher, 2,542 independent bookstores have survived across the country in 2019, despite the bookstore slaughter perpetrated by Amazon.com over recent years.

Their employees displaced in the workplace, many store owners also most likely became bankrupt. How many will find new jobs, how many can be retrained, how many businesspeople can start anew? Many social traditions of personal contact will disappear. All this weakens our society's cohesion at a time when cohesion is what we need to strengthen optimism, confidence, and hence resilience.

To digress, bookstores (and libraries) tell us about our community spirit. Neither are solely about books but rather serve as meeting places of the like-minded concerning our culture. The commerce aspect here is not of the essence. Good for resilience.

Foreign commerce

The consequences of covid-19 and of ex-president Trump's tariff wars have brought changing foreign trade conditions. They center on gigantic China. The coronavirus events have focused the world's attention on the risks of depending on one country, China, for the sole supply of some essential drugs, such as capreomycin and streptomycin, both used to treat tuberculosis, and sulfadiazine, used to treat sexually transmitted diseases and trachoma. China also holds a near-monopoly of the production of rare earths, indispensable to the manufacture of electronic technology. In response, the American economy will diversify its suppliers and shorten its supply lines (to the probable advantage of Mexico). It may also repatriate the manufacture of critical drugs and intensify mining of rare earths, which appear to exist in abundance in the American West, though more costly to produce than in China. All this should create a modest boost in employment and be favorable for resilience.

Public health

The healthcare industry comprises the largest single component of the American economy—18% of the GDP and growing, the highest such ratio in the world.[7] Beyond the employment numbers discussed above, public health requires special attention for several reasons. Among them, epidemiology stands out because we can reasonably expect covid-19 to be a precursor of further epidemics. Also, because in public health, the economy meets culture and public policy on the largest scale.

The health sector includes direct medical costs but more broadly also the public health consequences of epidemics, drug overdoses, fires, floods, hurricanes, tornadoes, pollution, and earthquakes. Some of these are acts of God; others are acts of us. All have economic consequences, and all require us to make personal and government-policy decisions. We need to anticipate and prevent further epidemics. We need to address the consequences of environmental disasters. And we must assume personal responsibility for our health as it affects our entire society, because we are accountable to our fellow citizens.

Epidemics

We need to view epidemics and their consequences as a recurring threat to our economy. Covid-19 and its ongoing mutations overhang our lives. It is the latest in a series of worldwide epidemics, and anything worldwide affects us too. We should see covid-19 as a link in a chain of viral attacks in just recent years. It was preceded by HIV/AIDS (1980), SARS (2002), MERS (2012), Ebola (2013), and Zika (2016), among others such as the avian flu and the swine flu.[8]

Logic and scientific evidence thus dictate that viral, epidemic attacks should continue. Nature has shown its persistent efforts and ability to maintain equilibrium in its system. When given a chance, it repairs the damage inflicted on it. Among myriad examples, we can think of the reintroduction of wolves in Yellowstone National Park that brought its entire ecosystem in balance, the banishment of certain pesticides that brought back large numbers of bald eagles, eucalyptus burned to a crisp in Australia's 2019 fires spurting green growth out of charred trunks. But when under particular strain, nature takes the offensive. Such, I believe, are the numberless virus armies it releases to tame our numbers and our abuses. It should not surprise us that SARS and covid-19 originated in China, the most massively overpopulated real estate on earth, and that its material growth places the most extreme distress on the natural equilibrium.

How we respond and adapt to the threat of epidemics will depend on our character. Will our instincts turn positive and hence resilient? Our culture will tell. To eliminate covid-19, for instance, or to at least reduce this danger, we need to vaccinate the majority of our population. Polls by the Pew Research Center indicate that 40% of Americans declared themselves antivaxxers in December 2020 (astounding that anyone would reject vaccination after more than two centuries of its successful application). If that proportion of the population doesn't accept vaccinations, covid-19 will linger through additional infections with the economic consequences that became familiar in 2020/2021—another example of the conflict between our economy's needs and our cultural attitudes, which I discuss under "Science" in chapter 6. Though social pressures may reduce the number of antivaxxers, this division among Americans weakens us.

Environment as public health

In how we deal with our environment, the economy and public health intertwine. Some treat the environment with reverence, some with indifference. Some heedlessly pollute air and water and waste vital resources. Powerful interests attempt oil exploration in the Arctic National Wildlife Refuge. A mindset bent on exploiting the environment as if we lived in an America of two hundred years ago. Such attitudes harm our health and hit our pocketbooks, as when we must clean polluted rivers and toxic dumps or are caused to drink poisoned water, as in Flint, Michigan. Other citizens, aghast, have sponsored laws, federal and state, to protect nature and a healthy environment. These differences in our views of the environment create hostility and incomprehension, yet another challenge to our coming together and restoking our capital of resilience.

Today's environmental concern centers on climatic warming. This elicits another source of passionate discord and carries enormous economic and public-policy implications. On climate, we need to take an informed, measured position between apocalyptics and outright deniers.

Incontrovertible evidence exists of warming taking place. How it will affect the United States is uncertain because we rely on scientifically shaky models.[9] The mathematics used to describe complex systems appear still inadequate to predict future conditions. So far, the warming has affected mostly the polar regions, with much ice melting, and the equatorial, with mild sea level rises in the Pacific and some glacier melting in subtropical ranges. How our economy, largely located in the middle latitudes, will be tested is as yet unclear. Nor do we know what public health effects it will have. If warming in fact causes intensified fires and more violent hurricanes, then the coming decades will exact an economic toll. But crops may respond favorably, especially in more northern latitudes.

If history is a guide, American ingenuity—often resulting from multitudes of individuals experimenting, tinkering, trying, and erring—will produce solutions to massive problems, time after time. They did it in 1942, transforming our economy in months to deal with World War II; in the Manhattan project; in flying to the moon. We are but in the infancy of solving the climate warming problem. Many solutions exist, some financial through taxation of emissions, some technological through adaptation to changing conditions. The American character has proven up to the task in the past.

Whatever the warming's effects, it will affect less the well-to-do and more the disadvantaged, economically and in terms of public health. It behooves us to implement strong and extensive environmental protection measures now. They will contribute to reducing warming of our climate. It's complex, and it needs a carefully thought-out public policy. I propose such in chapter 8, under "A balance-of-nature policy."

Our personal health responsibility

We hold a social responsibility for our personal health. When we undermine it through alcoholism, drug abuse, self-inflicted obesity-induced maladies, or smoking, we place health and economic burdens on our fellow citizens. Tragically, eighty-one thousand Americans died of a drug overdose in one year ending May 31, 2020—a disease of despair.[10] The economic costs mount through enormous medical expenses. How can deaths of despair, let alone on that scale, occur in this richest and most open to opportunity of countries? It's not new. Six decades ago, when I had just arrived in the United States, I worked in the port of New York. I walked every morning down the Bowery on my way to the docks. Dozens of men lay in drunken stupor on the sidewalks. It stunned me then, and I don't understand it still today. Do we not know how to make every American feel worthy?

How each one of us behaves affects us all. Any retreat from social responsibility opens another fissure as we quest to find common ground.

Entrepreneurial spirits and investor instincts

Economics, politics, or epidemics notwithstanding, the American can-do, gung-ho yearning for change, improvements, and innovation never seems to wane. The entrepreneurial spirits of Jeff Bezos's Amazon and Elon Musk's PayPal, SpaceX rocketry, and Tesla electric vehicles animate our current economy. Amazingly, the coronavirus year of 2020 saw a record of 480 IPOs (initial public stock offerings by new companies). That is 106% more than in 2019 and considerably surpasses the previous record of 397, set in 2000. The US Census Bureau reports that in 2020, 550,000 new business applications were submitted in various states. This exceeds the previous record, set in 2019, by 83%. During the dot-com implosion in 2000, the market suffered a meltdown. The Tech Wreck and the Dot-com Bubble took eight trillion dollars in wealth with them as they tanked the market. By 2004, the economy and the stock market had recovered. A troubled economy doesn't seem to dampen investor spirits.

The stock market insists on affirming the positive. Throughout the pandemic year 2020, it kept rising, indifferent to the realities of an economy at times in freefall. It continued trumpeting a bright future, at least as seen from Wall Street. What to conclude about investor optimism in troubled times? Is it savvy foreknowledge or innate American visceral positivism? A symptom of resilience?

But even in expansive entrepreneurial spirits, we can find cause for our nation's divisions. The Economic Innovation Group reported in September 2020 that entrepreneurs are migrating to large urban centers of economic vigor and deserting much of the country's medium and smaller towns. A metropolitan, entrepreneurial America and another America going their separate ways.

Let the economy be or give it a nudge?

The economy is an independent beast. It responds to countless random influences but obeys no rules. Many try to direct it, but it can defy the mandates of central bankers, disappoint sophisticated forecasts by economists, disregard government programs, and frustrate investors. We must decide how we shall manage it. Allow it to grow organically, driven by technology's successes and investors' exuberant spirits, but without other purpose than growth? More gross domestic product benefiting some but not all? Or try to tame

the best and nudge it to stimulate opportunity, hope, confidence, and optimism across *all* segments of our society?
Interventions into the economy lead to new government
policies, the domain of the next chapter, where I explore
statism, socialism, industrial policy, and other scary ideas.

Chapter 8

Governance, Policy, and Legislation

———— ◆ ————

With malice toward none, with charity for all . . .

—Abraham Lincoln

Governance

Can we govern this country so that all will be included and none feel excluded? No, of course not. But we sure can do a lot better than we have over recent years. It will not be easy. For starters, we are divided ideologically, culturally, and economically. Which augurs poorly for those reasons alone, in addition to numerous other obstacles confronting our governance today. How to govern effectively under such conditions for perceived fairness, for reconciliation, and to restore national confidence?

Divides

In importance, our divisions overwhelm all other challenges that face our governance in coming years. I have two aging friends. American 1 is a liberal Democrat. American 2 is a conservative Republican. They don't know each other. In a political conversation in 2020 with American 1, I told him that in my experience, I found the great majority of Americans to be decent people. He looked at me skeptically and said, "What about the South? Are there any decent people there, with all the segregation?"

In a political conversation in 2020 with American 2, I asked him why so many Americans voted for Trump. He told me, pointing passionately at his chin, "Because they're up to here with political correctness, diversity, and multiculturalism."

American 1 doesn't know any Republicans but was ready to condemn the entire South as lacking decent people. American 2 knows some liberals but doesn't trust them. He tells me about millions of citizens who, like him, resist accepting changes in our evolving culture, a culture that normally produces change as a matter of reflex. Why? Too many changes, too quick, too unpalatable?

A canyon separates two Americas. They don't speak to each other; they don't even try to know or understand one another. Each feels right and virtuous. In addition to American 1 and American 2, we have a great variety of other kinds of Americans, each with their own grievances and incomprehensions. They use different cultural languages, part from incompatible positions, and do not understand the reality of the country in the same way. We can't afford this because it makes balanced governing impossible. (I explore how we have come to that in the next chapter on the march of our culture.)

In addition to left/right politics, we also feud along tribal lines. Certainly, along the Black/White divide. That animus goes back centuries and remains often poisonous. Racial (that is, skin color) dislikes continue to generate extreme emotions. Under the broad White supremacist umbrella shelter other unfriendly sentiments like xenophobia and anti-Semitism, and not just the old-fashioned KKK. The left contributes its inflammatory share, and the tearing down of Confederate statues certainly adds to hostility. American 1 typifies intransigent self-righteousness on the left.

White grievances seem ineradicable today, but they have actually become dated. They drive principally, though not exclusively, middle-aged and older individuals. The mob that stormed the US Capitol on January 6, 2021, contained many self-described White supremacists. They were middle-aged and even older, not young, as one would expect from an enraged mob.

Meanwhile, we had a Black president (which ignited some passions), two Black secretaries of state, a Black defense secretary, and a Black Catholic cardinal, to mention a few distinguished Blacks. We also have millions of Black college graduates and professionals, all of whom now belong financially to a middle stratum, or better, of our society. Should we continue to see them as "Black" or as Americans with just darker skin? The young college graduates with whom I speak seem to incline toward the latter. The US Constitution says (obliquely) that we are all equal. Can we rally today around America as an idea, not as the purview of a single ethnicity? I think it significant that I encounter young college graduates or college students who hold benign views on race. They were born twenty to twenty-five years ago, are third-generation or more college-educated, and were exposed to multitudes of ideas at home, in school, and through a profusion of media. They represent the generational replacement in our culture's evolution I write about in earlier chapters. Their emergence will ease the burdens of governance.

We also allow a cultural-geographic antagonism to fester. As the Obama-Trump years have shown, large portions of the White South remain, nearly 160 years after the Civil War, a separate political and cultural unit, often suspicious of northern condescension. It votes by and large accordingly. "The past," William Faulkner said, "is never dead. It's not even past."

Overlaying this by now traditional North-South divide, we witness the emergence of a pronounced new geographic separation. Smaller towns and rural communities increasingly diverge culturally and economically from large metropolises. Small-town America mostly retains a laudable, traditional community spirit that defines its values all too often in opposition to those of metropolitan America.

And votes accordingly. Small towns are also losing many young who migrate to the big, dynamic cities, where seemingly alien behaviors reign. Enlightened governance needs to urgently address economic and political consequences of this growing separation. That will not be easy because these changes rise from the whirlwind of accelerating modernity.

Compounding divisions, we find an economy unequally distributed. We saw in chapter 7 how technology has marginalized a huge segment of our population—those with only a high-school diploma or with other educational limitations. They don't participate in the high-tech- and science-driven prosperity of those benefiting from a transformed workplace. Disparities in economic wellbeing have sprung from this division.

The super divider

Without social media, all our divisions would not be so categorical. This phenomenon has changed our society profoundly. Undoubtedly, social media offers benefits. Families and friends can communicate frequently. Business and government functions are rendered more effective. The most unexpected information has become available. But the damage it inflicts on all of us has yet to be accounted for.

In January 2021, I received over social media a stream of very funny anti-Trump cartoons. It came to me as an unwitting member of the tribe into which algorithms have placed me. As we laughed at the humor, I asked myself, "What about the seventy-four million who voted for Trump in 2020? Do they laugh?" Assuredly not, but we don't know that because social media has aggregated us into separate markets.

Facebook's, Google's, or Twitter's algorithms categorize us by what they can sell us. We click on this, we click on that, and in the end, all messages reach us filtered, placing us politically into one tribe and not the other.

Social media separates us, but more, it actively harms us. It allows violent, criminal, or extremist groups to communicate, organize, and recruit clandestinely and anonymously through advanced encryption methods. It allows unexamined, misleading, or outright untruthful propaganda to reach a public all too often lacking in critical judgment. Without social media, ISIS would not have taken off, nor would some domestic, hard-right, violent groups. Social media allows the formation of antisocial communities. Thus divided, millions of Americans watch only partisan TV channels. But we must govern for all.

Obstacles

How to govern under such conditions? American governance strides into mighty headwinds in the 2020s:

It must govern a country divided in so many distinct and antagonistic ways.

It must do it in a population of 331 million vastly diverse people, which doesn't enable it to allot individual attention to any of them so as to promote the good or to prevent the evil. (Well, maybe the ultrarich political donors may get a larger smidgen of personal attention.)

It must do it despite the power of government constitutionally moderated by the division between federal and state. The covid-19 crisis demonstrated in 2020 the difficulties of coordinating the different levels of government under the political peculiarities of our constitutional arrangement.

It must do it as technology disrupts employment, transforms the economy vertiginously, and unbalances society through social media.

Add domestic terrorism, a cancer on our culture. Add cybercrime, domestic and foreign, threatening our infrastructure, our banks, and the very functioning of government itself. Throw in mass shootings, the effects of novel scientific and technical developments, or cryptocurrencies. All have far-reaching consequences for how we govern our country.

Quite a menu. So how to establish common goals, beliefs, and values that would permit governing effectively and equitably for all? Not to mention cultivating national resilience. Let's consider needed policies.

Policy

Here I propose five policies that form the core long-term concerns of our governance: education, immigration, the economy, the preservation of natural systems, and the strengthening of our communities. Each will encounter stiff resistances for reasons of culture, politics, and ingrained habits.

I am writing this during the Biden administration. President Biden has proposed an avalanche of legislation. It aims at the problems of his day, as defined by the Democratic Party. That is not my aim. The policies I propose are long-range, aspirational, and nonpartisan in their intent. My horizon stretches into the next three or four decades. It aims to guide us to a common center, where confidence meets optimism and where together they evolve into resilience.

I have approached the writing of this book without strong preconceptions about government's role in supporting our resilience. As my writing progressed, my mind changed, influenced by demography. I came to America appreciating the relatively limited range and power of the government and its distributed character between federal and the state. In 1960, there were 189 million Americans, somewhat over a half of their present number. At its birth, with fewer than four million people, the fledgling nation could afford the luxury of limited government. Even at the turn of the twentieth century, in Teddy Roosevelt's days, there were only seventy-six million.

The size and diversity of our present population and the complexity and world-importance of our economy do not allow reduced government anymore. A small government today is an illusion and a romantic fantasy about our simpler past. Under our current circumstances, I have reluctantly come to the conclusion that we need a strengthened and expanded federal government.

With that statement, I enter dangerous territory. More government may mean statism, defined as concentration of economic controls and planning in the hands of a highly centralized state, often extending to its ownership of industry. It may also mean socialism, defined as governmental ownership and administration of the means of production and distribution of goods, as well as a certain level of social paternalism. Or it may mean industrial policy, defined as organized government involvement in guiding the economy by encouraging investment in targeted industries. Such horrors run counter to the American spirit, and none of them we want.

Yet the United States has practiced mild forms of industrial policy over the past century. In a stricter form, it interferes with the free flow of private initiative, the lifeblood of our economy. Our commitment to open and free markets made this country rich and powerful. But novel times demand novel thinking and, with that, new targeted policies to relieve blockages and strengthen our institutions. Circumstances arise when technical misjudgment, a quest for short-term profits, or plain neglect leads to critical national security consequences.

> Computer chips run our digital world—that is, the modern world. They allow us to use our cars, our smartphones, in fact our entire computer-dependent society. Critically, our military needs them to operate its tanks, airplanes, surface ships, and submarines. Americans invented computer chips. Intel, once the queen of Silicon Valley, reigned supreme over the computer chips world market as recently as twenty years ago. Then we allowed chip manufacture to move abroad, primarily to Taiwan. Now the Taiwan Semiconductor Manufacturing Company (TSMC) controls 84% of the computer chip

> market and Intel maybe 2%. TSMC not only
> leads the world in chip sales, but at this
> writing its chips are also two generations
> more advanced than others on the market.
> Other than Intel in decline, the United States
> has few other significant computer chip
> manufacturers. And we buy most of our
> chips from TSMC. What if China invaded
> Taiwan? It could bring our economy to its
> knees. It's a national security matter.[1]

In this case, I back off any reservations about the role of government. It's a threat to our nation, and the national government must direct industry. Such instances should be exceptional. In the main, the fine art of enlightened policy must remain human in scale, humane in character, and not lapse into bureaucratic invasiveness.

The American Dream

We hear much talk about the death of the American Dream and how our society no longer offers opportunity for all to achieve it. To ensure the survival and prospering of the American Dream, we need to put together policies in the five areas I list above: education, immigration, economy, care of natural systems, and fostering of the community.

An education policy

In formulating the new education policy, Congress and the executive branch need to base it on the following realities: Our knowledge-based future depends as never before on greatly improved education. Our present system, based on a weak federal mandate and a chaotic diversity of standards in some 26,400 community school districts, has resulted in an educational bankruptcy that has landed us thirty-fourth in the world in 2015. In chapter 5, I describe the problem in detail. To come to grips with the damage, we must transit from the nineteenth century into the twenty-first in one revolutionary swoop.

A) Congress must greatly increase the mandate of the federal Department of Education. The DOE should establish common national public education goals (not a rigid, mandated curriculum), control and enforce them, and provide the system with thoughtfully targeted, expansive funding. This will require a radical change in taxation, because the current system depends heavily on local taxes. That creates vast differences in educational outcome, dependent on wealth or its absence. The new financial model would allow numerous universal improvements. An example would be the provision of a laptop or equivalent with Wi-Fi available to every learner in public schools.[2]

B) Congress should mandate a universal, well-funded minds-enrichment program at the earliest, pre-K ages to compensate for disparities in mental readiness of children of diverse backgrounds. In earlier chapters, I have devoted priority attention to secondary education because of the abundance of available data. What happens in high school results from infancy years and certainly by preschool. Solid funding should continue through kindergarten and beyond so that all children reach the first grade with a comparable degree of mental readiness.

In recent years, a bipartisan Congress has kept modestly increasing funding of preschool. Thus in 2020, the House budget contained $22.6 billion for various programs to this end—a timid increase of fifty-one million dollars over 2019. The Senate balked at such profligacy and cut into it. The First Five Years Fund and a number of other concerned organizations call on Congress to significantly increase funding of specific needs. The new education policy must respond full bore. Today's children are our common future. We need to conceptualize it as a matter of national interest, not as some governmental welfare project.

C) Congress should foment and fund an ambitious program of technical training. We have millions of jobs to fill in technical fields (see chapter 7 under "Employment"). Secondary and postsecondary education policy should reevaluate the current strong predilection for college for all. Many young people are not intellectually inclined but would greatly profit from an advanced preparation in skills not requiring four years of college.

D) As discussed in more detail in chapter 5, the new policy should entirely revamp our teacher education and recruitment system. Schools of education should become staffed mainly with PhD faculty, steeped in subject matter competence covering the entire academic spectrum and not solely by EdDs trained in teaching methods, not in subjects. Raised standards of schools of education should produce a much higher caliber corps of (well-compensated) teachers.

E) The upgraded profession should lead to a reappraisal of the role of teachers unions. The new policy should promote their transformation from self-protecting, quasi-industrial unions into professional associations in recognition that teaching the young is the most important of professions.

To those attached to the past, these recommendations may seem an unacceptable departure from a tradition of separation between federal governance and assertion of individual communities. But so are Social Security, Medicare, and federal taxes. We accept them because commonsense needs dictate them. So let's do it for education. We need to raise our sights considerably; thirty-fourth will not do. It is, in fact, shameful.

An immigration policy

In formulating this new immigration policy, Congress and the executive branch need to base it on the following realities:

Immigrants built this country. The United States today is the result of their labors. This stands as our guiding principle, an idea that we must constantly rekindle like an eternal flame. In chapter 4, I discuss my concerns that all too many present-day descendants of immigrants have forgotten this principle and the ethic it has produced. While guided by that principle and that ethic, a new immigration policy must also reflect our present needs. Today's immigration priorities must focus on employment and demography.

A) The new policy needs to recognize the various levels of employment our economy requires. We need the well-educated. Especially, though not exclusively, those trained in in the STEM fields. Of these, we have great needs. SmartBrief Education Originals reports that in 2018, we had potentially twenty-four million unfilled positions in the STEM fields. This is a huge gap: in 2019, these professions employed some 10.7 million. We also need skilled technicians in a variety of modern jobs. At the other end of the employment spectrum, we need a certain number who, while little educated, can take essential jobs in fields like agriculture and construction spurned by the native-born in our exceedingly prosperous society. The new policy should institute a system of periodic reviews of our economic needs.

B) Demographically, we want them all young and fertile to allow us to maintain a replacement birth rate of 2.1 children per mother. An optimistic, resilient society requires demographic stability. Our new policy should endeavor that we don't fall into a depressing demographic decline like those affecting Europe, South Korea, Japan, and other prosperous countries. We need a constant supply of young to support a large cohort of aging retirees.

C) In accordance with the American character's responsive nature, the new policy should allow for admission of qualified political refugees out of humanitarian considerations. There should be no quotas, but admissions would require careful due process to determine that the applicants meet strict criteria.

Let's make them all feel welcome! But let's formulate the new policy thoughtfully. The very mention of immigrants raises reflexive hackles in a large segment of less-educated natives. Donald Trump's 2016 campaign leaned heavily on immigrant exclusion (of Muslims, Mexican wall, etc.). Inevitably, many new immigrants in the twenty-first century will often have darker skin and bring untraditional (to us) religious practices. The new policy needs to meet two simultaneous objectives: it must educate skeptical natives about its benefits, and it must appeal to and attract prospective immigrants. To the natives, it must explain that all new entrants will come under strictly controlled legal procedures and that they will benefit us all by filling needed employment spots and strengthening our demographic prospects. This policy should provide incentives for immigrant assimilation. It will all take some educating.

A policy for an economy in transition

In formulating a new economic policy, Congress and the executive branch need to base it on the following realities:

During the covid-19-afflicted year 2020, the stock market raced ever upward, seemingly undeterred by the troubled economy. Just a few high-tech giants like Amazon, Apple, Facebook, Google, Microsoft, Netflix, Tesla, and Twitter stoked the market's giddy performance. This concealed the reality of the rather negligible contribution of the rest of the economy to the stock market's success. In chapter 7, we saw how high tech selectively rearranges our economy. It favors the well prepared and disappoints, or worse, the unprepared.

A) Open competition stimulates creative juices and, so, is resilience's partner. To keep a vigorous economy, the new policy must favor open markets and guard against potential monopolies, lest they strangle competition. This will call for balance. High-tech giants at present exhibit monopolistic tendencies by buying up potential competitors. Still, we can anticipate great benefits from tech-driven developments. Multiple efficiencies created by automation, online commerce, and robots will result in economies and unprecedented conveniences for the consumer and in growing profits for (surviving) businesses. The new policy must place no obstacles to the freedom to innovate (and to destroy). It's the American genius. We should regulate gingerly for fear of stifling initiative and innovation. And we should fear the consequences of protectionism.

B) Small businesses represent 44% our economic activity.[3] Consequences of automation and covid-19 fall heaviest on that sector. Disruptions include the displacement of workers, the erosion of employment, and the essential necessity to retrain human capital. The new policy must address all that and also reposition small business owners and restimulate their entrepreneurial energies. It must also decide how to handle physical plants fallen into disuse, including entire shopping malls.

C) The new policy will need to anticipate consequences of likely changes and innovations, particularly multiple unanticipated business disruptions caused by high tech's progress in automation and online commerce. In chapter 7, I describe the demise of Blockbuster. That company never anticipated the arrival of Netflix, and once confronted by its appearance, Blockbuster failed to appreciate its significance. That ability to anticipate the unforeseeable is a government function too. For instance, it modernizes our armed forces, just in case. With technology's vast effect on the economy, public policy must take an equally anticipatory approach by watching ongoing trends or unexpected developments (terrorist uses of the internet, dangerous abuses of genetic engineering).

A balance-of-nature policy

In formulating a new environment policy, Congress and the executive branch need to base it on the following realities:

The American public values nature. If formulated from that perspective, a new policy should receive strong public support. Multimillions of us hold our national parks—an American invention—in strong personal esteem. We reintroduced the wolf into Yellowstone some forty years ago from Canada after we had nearly exterminated it in the lower forty-eight states. It has now reestablished the balance of nature in the park. When the bald eagle neared extinction sixty years ago, we banned DDT, and our national bird soars again. The shad was an extraordinarily abundant fish in the mid-Atlantic rivers. By the 1960s and '70s, it had almost disappeared from the Potomac. But Americans cleaned the river and established hatcheries, and the shad is back in full strength in the clean river. Some advocate eliminating the western national parks so that they can exploit the natural resources therein. Let them try!

A) The new policy should aim to unite us in a commitment to nature's balance. Talk of climate warming or of environment generally quickly turns political and hence divisive. A new policy needs to change the terms of the discourse by focusing on maintaining the balance of nature's systems. This is a vast educational function to which government must commit itself. The pressing goal is, once more,

to educate us to think differently. We need to take con-
science that nature, when in balance, allows life to function
harmoniously. No one seems to find controversial that
female and male babies are born in more or less equal proportion. This balance—a law of nature—has lasted, generation after generation, for millions of years. So why should
caring for nature's balance in all its other manifestations
elicit controversy?

The mental consensus I advocate will be extremely difficult to achieve at this advanced stage of our political
discord. Al Gore, with his sarcastic *An Inconvenient Truth,* has
caused lasting damage because he politicized an otherwise
common-good issue. The new policy must at all costs avoid
making nature a matter of politics. That closes dialogue.
Steven Koonin, in *Unsettled,* makes a careful argument for
a data-based, politically disimpassioned consideration of
climate change and for a rational management of our relationship with nature.[4]

B) The new policy should offer incentives for nature-bal-
ance-conscious behaviors. This means all the obvious:
preserve and protect the existing natural systems, waste
not, pollute not, do not overuse limited resources (critically
water), and do not contribute individually or societally to the
warming of the climate. Promote advanced solar, wind, and
latest, safer nuclear technologies. Not for ideological reasons
but because we all live in this country and want our life envi-
ronmentally clean and harmonious.

A policy for fostering the community

In formulating a new community policy, Congress and the executive branch need to recognize the following realities:

The above policy is about how we coexist with nature. This one is about how we coexist with each other. We are as divided as we were in 1860. That didn't end well. Today, millions of Americans believe that the November 2020 election was fraudulent and that its winner stole it. Their belief is not based on any facts, just unsupported assertions. This, folks, is a crisis, not only of the mechanisms of democracy but of our society itself. We cannot go on like this. It's time to repair.

How to reverse and rebuild? Reviving our community spirit seems the most promising strategy to combat our social isolations and political divisions. I keep repeating my story about Paradise, a small town in California's Central Valley that got reduced to cinders in an enormous wildfire in 2018. Within hours, people from an extended geographic implicit community began arriving unbidden to help. Some came from as far as fifty miles. None asked whether the fire's victims were Democrats or Republicans. They saw fellow Americans in distress, and they helped. That spirit, which we inherited from pioneering ancestors, survives but seemingly only flickers in larger cities with mobile populations.

Many factors have contributed over recent decades to undermine the community. Migration from abroad or from smaller heartland towns to large cities certainly did. It is hard to establish a neighborly feeling in a megalopolis with constantly renewing populations in motion. Compartmentalizations according to wealth or its absence, by ethnicity, by education, and other social factors predominate in large conurbations with their suburbs.

In 2020, the mayor of Paris, Anne Hidalgo, introduced a policy to promote community-building. The policy's goal is to ensure that all residents of Paris live within fifteen minutes' walking or cycling of their daily activities, such as general shopping, banking, healthcare facilities, police, and city administration. This creates neighborhoods where people meet face to face instead of undertaking long, solitary journeys by metro or car to achieve their daily objectives. Streets are being pedestrianized, cars banished, bicycles encouraged. We'll have to see how that works on rainy days or in winter, but other European cities follow Paris's lead. Rain gear sales should boom.

Is such an urban revolution possible in American cities? Possibly in some. The main community underminers are, however, Facebook and other social media. Their algorithms slice and dice us into online, mutually exclusive communities. Our neighbor may be next door, but we may be cultural algorithms apart. Now, surely, we have in the US Congress 535 brilliant, insightful minds, unencumbered by considerations of personal interest (ahem), capable of devising a series of community-building measures. Such as:

A) Social media once more. Foremost, Congress can regulate a stop to social media's splitting activities, separating us into partisan online communities. Algorithms that provide for successful business outcomes are, of course, indispensable for the economy to prosper. But the companies that generate such algorithms have implicit civic responsibilities. Enlightened policies can cause American ingenuity to control the effects of divisive technology. Deprived of fuel, acute partisan fires may abate. Then the places where we live may become communities without acerbity. See, below, the section about legislation.

B) Volunteerism. The community spirit lives endemic in this country, expressed in abundant volunteerism, even in large metropolitan areas. The Corporation for National and Community Service reported in November 2018 that more than seventy-seven million American adults (a record) volunteered through a community organization in the preceding twelve months. The new policy needs to stimulate this rich cultural reservoir in large cities, where it may lie more dormant than in the heartlandd's towns.

C) National service. Congress should mandate a universal national service for *all* young people, including rich papas' daughters and sons. The goal is to cause all the young to mingle for a year or two with a full cross-section of Americans. Options are infinite: military service for some, limitless civilian activities for many. Teaching, health-care services, infrastructure revitalization, nature-balance preservation, among numerous other needs of our society.

Through a universal national service, the young acquire diverse and valuable life experiences and get to know other Americans whose lives and communities they would otherwise ignore. To this end, an essential requirement is that the young *not* serve in their own community. We experienced the value of such service in the Civilian Conservation Corps in the 1930s, in the Peace Corps, and in AmeriCorps. Let's require it for all and make it useful and individually valuable. Who will object? We'll see.

Priority legislation

These five policy proposals have the aspirational purpose to improve our society. A multitude of laws may result from their implementation. Meanwhile, we require immediate legislation to address concerns that we cannot postpone:

- Rebuild and modernize our workforce.

- Bring under control the internet and social media.

- Ban firearms in dangerous times.

Rebuild and modernize our workforce. The government (let's remember, it's all of us) must step in massively with programs worthy of an enlightened society. It stepped in during the 1930s to stave off an economic crisis, and in 1944 with the GI Bill, to open the doors of prosperity for very many. Today, the time has come for Congress to enact several crucial bills.

Rebuilding the Workforce Bill. An equivalent of the GI Bill, this will be strongly led and funded by the federal government for a massive education, re-education, and training of those left behind and those displaced. In this moment in the twenty-first century, we must make brave decisions, devoid of dated small-government ideologies, and show faith in our future. We can continue to strengthen this country by building its human capital.

Bring under control the internet and social media. As I indicate in earlier chapters, an uncontrolled internet provides many benefits but also increases societal harm. We need to judiciously control it now.

Social Media Responsibilities Bill. Congress must confront without delay the danger of unhindered access to electronic mayhem by internet-driven crime and subversion. Malefactors mislead and confuse the citizenry or ransom businesses and government. Terrorist organizations, domestic and foreign, use encrypted messaging to radicalize and recruit, to distribute propaganda, to sponsor would-be terrorists' training, and to commit acts of terror. Artificial intelligence makes these operations more dangerous and better targeted by allowing them to build frightening weapons like killer robots and silent, hovering drones.[5] This bill must specify the responsibilities of the social media companies to society. This calls for very difficult and delicate legislation, because we must keep the First Amendment as an incorruptible beacon and preserve the openness of our civic life. Yet we cannot allow abuses of our constitutional liberties. The penalties for breaching this law should be very consequential. No monetary fines, which are laughable to these economic giants. Jailing individuals and breaking up the companies will concentrate agile minds.

Mark Zuckerberg created Facebook; Mark Zuckerberg is responsible for all consequences.

Ban firearms in dangerous times. The news reports mass shootings several times each month as a matter of routine. We can no longer shrug. The shootings must stop.

Firearms in the Twenty-First Century Bill. Ban guns. Yes, I know, these two words produce an emotional volcano of indignation. But we certainly can regulate who, under what conditions, can own certain classes of arms. The basic argument of those who want no change in the present situation is that if we ban guns, only criminals would have them. That's obfuscation. Criminals already have them. Law-abiding citizens have them mostly secured so that they won't have a chance to use them against criminals. (Yes, there are exceptions.) Yet, today, a mentally unstable, irresponsible individual or a political fanatic can get hold of weapons of mass killing. Is that the aim of the Second Amendment? This isn't colonial America anymore, and it's time to abandon archaic fantasies and join the realities of the twenty-first century.

Today, we harbor dangers that current policies don't address. We have criminals, we have the unstable, and we have small subpopulations who are radically disaffected from society's mainstream. In their anger, all can inflict catastrophic damage with unprecedented means through a limitless supply of advanced weapons of war. The news regularly reports mass murders in our schools, churches, synagogues, malls, and theaters. Our culture, in its seemingly boundless affection for guns, allows these dangers to persist. (More on this in appendix 3.)

Congress must face up today to a seemingly impossible task. It needs to gird its loins and do the impossible (the impossible, we know, just takes a little longer in America). This bill must specify who has the right to own a firearm, of what kind, under what conditions, for what purpose. Penalties for breaches of this law should be appropriately severe. We're dealing with the safety of our people.

These three bills are, of course, good governance issues concerning acute present conditions of our society. Unresolved, they sap confidence and resilience and therefore constitute a priority for Congress to legislate.

Policy and statesmanship

We live in inconceivable times; it's time to adopt inconceivable measures. The policies I propose call for nonpartisan statesmanship. To craft such policies, congressional minds will need to shed sharp habits and convert to a goodwill bipartisanship. A distant goal—a fantasy, perhaps—in the existing climate of the present-day Congress but not necessarily in the public at large. Statesmen (of either sex) lead us, but politicians only follow us. Can we, the public, muster statesmanship? Can we cause our representatives to exhibit the requisite courage and patriotism in the coming years? Maybe. In World War II, Americans came together, and even statesmen like George Marshall emerged. Perhaps it will take a great crisis—larger than the four shocks described in this book. A moment when We the People will assume responsibility for our governance. A test of America the Exceptional, a nation that rules itself, not ruled from above.

Chapter 9

The March of Our Culture

———— ♦ ————

In March and April 2020, when evidence of the severity of covid-19 hit public consciousness, an emotional buying spree erupted in America. Grocery shelves were emptied. Among the largest early purchases were toilet paper and guns. Toilet paper and guns? To shoot the coronavirus or to wipe it out?

Who are these shelf strippers? What motivates their fears? Do they belong to a subculture? Does such panic behavior diagnose the fragile state of our culture in the home of the brave and of the resilient? Has the coronavirus caught us mentally unprepared for life's at times fatal unpredictability? Over recent decades, our culture has absorbed an ever-accelerating whirlwind of change. Has this tension disoriented us? Softened us? Have we drifted away from a character largely strong and unified during World War II? Or does the core of our culture remain solidly anchored?

Each of these questions bears on the state of our resilience, the central objective of this inquiry. Four elements appear to principally influence and even define the march of our culture in the third decade of the twenty-first century:

- The disconcerting rapidity of *computer technology*-induced change

- The d*emographics* of ethno-racial commotions, of aging, and of our geographic distribution

- An increasingly *uneven sharing of prosperity*

- Our *cleavages*, particularly political polarization and its cultural roots

Where does the combined effect of all this turbulence leave us? Timorous, confident, optimistic, pessimistic, uncertain?

The internet's influence

Could they have done that twenty-five years ago? For each of the following situations, let's ask that question.

- A woman walks down the street speaking into her phone. So does a man while checking out at a grocery store and then paying with the same phone.

- Without leaving home, a consumer orders just about anything online and has it delivered in twenty-four hours.

- A politician summons crowds of supporters on Twitter in a matter of minutes.

- Teenagers are glued to their phones for hours seeking approval on Facebook, Instagram, or TikTok.

- A couple on a date in a restaurant: she communicates with her smartphone; he communicates with his. Neither communicates with each other.

- An executive working from home doesn't need to commute to the office. Zoom does fine.

- Terrorists and criminals, domestic and foreign, recruit, organize, and plot mayhem with encrypted email.

- Both the youth and the adults engage in electronic distance learning.

- Social media messages spread wild rumors about the dangers of getting vaccinated.

- Two recent books[1] detail campaigns of disinformation by the Russian government using social media, an American invention, to undermine Americans' faith in their government and in democracy during the 2016 electoral campaign.

- A policeman kills a Black man in Minneapolis. A witness films it. Within hours, it goes viral and generates a vigorous, at times violent, agitation across the country, across the world.

- News appears on our screens every few minutes, novel, unexpected, puzzling, distressing, neutrally informative, pleasing misinformation often tinged with partisanship—all so fast that we have no time to absorb and digest the latest before it is replaced by more of the unimagined.

- That and so much more for free or next to free. Visual communications across the globe, facial recognition that shrinks the boundaries of our privacy, autonomous vehicles, cryptocurrencies, to name a few that surprise, amaze, disconcert, delight, and concern.

Yes, twenty-five years ago we couldn't do any of those things or, in fact, even imagine them. Some of it is actually good. Some, actually bad. Has the massive cumulative effect of internet technologies changed our culture? Changed us? Does the needle of our cultural compass in consequence wobble, or does it still point firmly north?

Demography

Majority/minority

As our population's ethnic diversity increases, the resulting ethno-racial changes upset many Whites. The US

Census Bureau and other sources[2] variously predict that between the 2040s and the 2060s, non-Hispanic Whites will become a minority and that the combined other ethnicities will become the majority of our population. Therefore, the formula minority/majority. The Census Bureau's projections, which predict a White minority by the mid-2040s, receive wide media publicity because they come from an official government agency. This stirs much White anxiety and translates into politics.

A significant portion of our White population, influenced by the bureau's projections, has grown increasingly worried about a perceived reduction of the Anglo-Saxon culture that "made America great" and that they regard as their birthright. I, too, consider our Anglo-Saxon origins the essential base of American culture and, in fact, immigrated because of it. Those worried about its loss believe that Anglo-Saxon culture somehow pertains solely to Non-Hispanic Whites. That is erroneous in my opinion: that culture expresses universal values and Americans of all skin hues practice it. Whites concerned with the loss of that culture voted massively for Trump Republicans in 2016 and 2020. From such anxieties, malignant outgrowths sprouted in the form of White supremacists and other extremist groupings. Conversely, other Whites, most Blacks, and many other ethnicities voted for Democrats. This part of the electorate favors expansive and inclusive demographics—another stark division among Americans.

The preceding raises questions. Are the majority/minority projections correct? Why should that matter? In its reports, the Census Bureau often yields to political pressures from those zealous about civil rights. This causes the bureau to create multiple classifications that don't always reflect common sense but distort our perceptions of the social reality.[3] Let's examine three cases.

Case 1: Half Latino. In chapter 4 on immigration, I speak of Adriana, a Nicaraguan who, with her husband, raised three daughters in the United States. I didn't mention that both she and her husband are White by any visual criterion. Their very well-educated daughters have married non-Hispanic White American men. All have children. The US Census classifies these children as Hispanic.

Case 2: All Latino. Isabel, a Mexican, the second lady I speak of in chapter 4, and her husband are both white-skinned but have clearly "Latino" physiognomies. They have raised three sons, all of whom finished college and married similar light-skinned Mexican-American young women. All appear White to the casual observer. They have children, born in the United States. The Census Bureau classifies these children as Hispanic.

Case 3: Half Asian. I have a friend, a very well-educated young woman. Her father is Austrian, her mother Japanese. My friend's physiognomy has only a slight hint of Asian, and she looks and acts as a typical "White" American. The Census Bureau classifies her as Asian.

A dream. A glorious day will come when no one will care about the census classifications anymore and when all of us will see each other as Americans, not as "ethnics." Most Mexicans we meet in the United States have light skin. If they were reclassified as White, that alone could extend the "White" majority by decades. Studies of friendship formations among high-school adolescents indicate that 50% of Hispanic students make friends with Whites, while another 13% make friends with "light-skinned" Hispanics. So much, it would seem, for the census classifications.

Of course, skin color is one factor, cultural assimilation quite another. Jeb Bush, former governor and presidential candidate, son and brother of American presidents, married a young Mexican woman. They have three children and several grandchildren. According to its rules, the US Census should classify these children and grandchildren as Hispanics. Are they not just Americans? Should the somewhat darker shade of their white skin make a difference? Or do they get a pass for who Jeb Bush is?

Furthermore, in 2019, 10% of babies born in the United States were of mixed ethnicity, like Jeb Bush's children. When one of the parents is White, by what criterion would the baby be classified to another race? We can conjure diverse scenarios. An excellent, in-depth discussion of the complexity of our population mixes appears in *The Great Demographic Illusion, Majority, Minority and the Expanding American Mainstream*, by Richard Alba (2020).

As to whether any of that matters, as a (White) immigrant, I don't believe it should. This gets to the heart of what I pursue in this book—to peer into our future, whether resilient or not. Who are we today? Are we shaping a common country or one with many separations?

To repeat, the United States was founded not as the purview of a specific ethnicity but as an idea of a society in which all citizens are free and are equal in their rights and obligations. (That this idea is breached daily and profusely by the weaknesses of human nature does not invalidate it in the least.) Of course, the country was created by an ethnicity whose language we speak and whose legal principles we practice. That ethnicity has given us its culture. Millions of immigrants from all over the world have come here because of that culture, whether they understood it or not. It transforms us all into Americans, regardless of shades of skin.

Let's consider the four most recent American presidents. One was Anglo-Saxon White (G. W. Bush); one had a White Anglo mother and a father born speaking Swahili in Africa (Obama); one was of half-German, half-Scottish blood (Trump); the fourth, straight Irish (Biden).

We are all in the melting pot business here, folks. The next few decades will fully display it. Of course, many tradition-bound Whites don't think as I do. They are mostly middle-aged, as we can see in Trump rally videos. The young, however, seem to think differently, and they engage in a multiplicity of cross-ethnic marriages and child-creating activities. But it will take decades for the majority/minority anxieties to vanish. Which brings us to aging.

The aging of our population

The present cohort of aged Americans is on the whole the most prosperous, healthiest, best educated (29% have at least a four-year college degree), most active in our history. Only 9% are poor, Blacks, and Latinos bearing the heaviest burden of poverty. Many old are confined to nursing homes or suffer from dementia, but the great majority enjoy unprecedented levels of health, supported by the advances of modern medicine. Their average life span now stands at eighty-one years, women outliving men by some seven years. The aged over sixty-five form a large portion of the country's population—in 2019, ninety-five million, or 28%.

This cohort marks our culture more than any before. They still work (18% do), they volunteer in huge numbers in civic affairs and in politics, they write, they read, they study, they travel, they engage in sports, and they create.[4] My friends Jorge and Bob avidly consume knowledge. Both take a steady stream of college courses on subjects of personal interest that they didn't have time to pursue when they worked. They make valuable grandparents, particularly in a society in which both parents work or where only one is present. Clint Eastwood, at ninety in 2021, remains fully active and creative. He said that he doesn't "let the old man in."

Because of their vitality, these ninety-five million have an enormous effect on our society and our culture. Older people tend toward conservative, and many of the present cohort are disproportionately concerned with issues of majority/minority in that they act as guardians of the culturally traditional, not a bad thing in itself. But if we disregard some of their complaints about a changing world, products of selective memories, their collective energy, without precedent in history, sends a positive message of our culture's continued stability and, by inference, perhaps of unconscious resilience.

Where we live

Demography also plays out on yet another front: in our geographical distribution, which adds a further dimension to our divisions. Americans have always lived in different settings, in rural communities, in small and medium-sized tows, in metropolises. In a fairly homogeneous culture, it didn't seem to make a significant difference. No longer. Small-town and big-city Americans march into the twenty-first century to rhythms of different fifes. From smaller communities, many depart for education, for opportunity, for personal reasons, never to come back. Few arrive into these communities from the outside. So, there, the culture remains rather constant, little disturbed by the goings on in San Francisco, of which they don't necessarily approve.

By contrast, large cities like New York, Los Angeles, Atlanta, Minneapolis, and a dozen or so others gather populations in social and cultural transition. The educated and the highly trained, the creative, and a great diversity of ethnicities live in cauldrons of change. Here the culture percolates.

The Research Triangle Park in North Carolina was conceived in 1959 to pool the intellectual creativity of three local universities. The park sits between three medium-size to small cities in the heart of the state: Raleigh, Durham, and Chapel Hill. Each has a large, distinguished university. The Research Triangle provides a magnet for innovative talents in a state of otherwise smaller communities (with the exception of large Charlotte). Culturally, the triangle is an island. It votes predominantly Democratic. The rest of the state votes predominantly Republican, with again the exception of large Charlotte.

Joel Kotkin, a demographer, has another take on the geography of our differences.[5] He divides the United States into places where people make and where they don't. The former are places with agriculture, heavy manufacturing, and energy extraction, such as oil drilling and fracking. Such places depend on hydrocarbons in one form or another. The workers hold well-paying jobs. Their culture lives in the present. But in the places where people don't make, the culture runs off into the future, into concerns about arising crises, especially in the environment and by extension about global warming and latent conflicts. They promote policies of renewable energies that would put out of work those who depend on hydrocarbons for a living. These two kinds of Americans, too, live in different places. Another geographical division translated onto our political map.

If, in fact, we look at the political map of the United States in the elections so far in the twenty-first century, we see that the blue states contain the great majority of large cities and the overwhelming majority of our best universities. Red states, with the exception of Texas, consist in contrast mostly of smaller communities, some predominantly rural, with few distinguished universities. This is meaningful because universities and cities attract those driven by knowledge, science, and modernity, open to new thinking and receptive to the culture's change and evolution. Those who don't fit well in culturally restricted environments leave. I reach such harsh conclusions reluctantly, but the maps don't lie. (Upper Midwest states, like Ohio, can swing to red or blue, depending on rust-belt economics, not so much on culture.)

The San Francisco Bay Area, with its seven million extremely diverse people, illustrates the political and cultural character of a churning blue metropolis. It covers numerous smaller communities and a couple of larger cities, all configured as an urban-suburban continuum and anchored by San Francisco, itself a moderate-sized city of some 700,000. The region contains three world-class universities: the University of California at Berkeley, the University of California of Health Sciences in San Francisco, and Stanford University. They power the intellectual, scientific, and technological prowess of the Bay Area, including Silicon Valley. The region attracts migration from the rest of the country and from the world. The culture simmers. The San Francisco Board of Education, in a paroxysm of political correctness, decided in 2021 to rename all forty-four schools in the city, changing the names of such questionable characters as Washington, Jefferson, Lincoln, and Paul Revere, among others. This upset many locals as our culture struggles to find a common point.

Prosperity

I should actually call this section "What is it about American prosperity that nags me?" Somehow this country's great affluence, as measured by the GDP and by simple observation, doesn't march in step with our culture. Prosperity should engender optimism, but that seems in short supply, partly victimized by covid-19 but mostly by deeper social causes.

That the super wealthy have too much doesn't trouble me. Let them enjoy it, particularly if their money was fairly acquired. It doesn't equate with happiness. That most Americans earn a decent living, have a roof over their head, have a car, can travel, have savings, and go to restaurants seems normal in this, the wealthiest of countries. That many Americans do not partake in the overall prosperity—that nags. In a resilient society, most all share in hope, optimism, and confidence. When significant portions of our population don't enjoy these feelings, it dims our prospects.

I see prosperity as a problem for our society for three reasons. The first is that too many Americans actually live in poverty, as defined by the US Census Bureau. In 2018, there were 38.1 million of them, amounting to some 13% of the population. This translated into one of every eight Americans living below the official poverty line. It affected 21% of Blacks, as well as 8% of non-Hispanic Whites, not to mention others, like Amerindians on reservations. We know the causes: endemic poverty in some segments of our society, lack of education, generations of out-of-wedlock births, broken or nonexistent families, and other social ills. We have much legislation that deals with the symptoms, but we can't find a way to attack the causes. This undermines, of course, our society's resilience.

A second reason for concern is that some fifty million Americans who have employment and live apparently well don't save for retirement. *Northwestern Mutual Planning & Progress Study* of 2019 reports that 15% of Americans had no savings at all for retirement. Do they feel confident and optimistic, or do they experience some financial anxiety about the thin base of their apparent wellbeing? Does our commercial culture push them to consume more than they need? Some, of course, earn so little that they cannot save for a rainy day or for retirement.

The third reason for concern is that too many feel left behind. Their factories closed, and their jobs flew off to China. With that, their unions vanished, and for many without a college education, the gates to prosperity closed. The culture has bifurcated. For the educated, the open gates beckon; for too many others, they have shut. So millions don't feel part of prospering America.

A Pew Research Center poll reports that 27% of Americans feel their financial condition is excellent, 48% that it is fair, and 24% that it is not (CNN Business, January 15, 2015). Only 27% in fabulously prosperous America feel fine? The great majority apparently do not. The 48% who report their condition as fair can be interpreted variously, but this doesn't seem to exude confidence. As for the 24% who poll as unsatisfactory, all too many of them live at the edge. As a result, many may not participate as active citizens in our civic life. Many suffer diseases and deaths of despair, especially on Indian reservations (they are Americans too) and in coal-mining Appalachia. The National Center for Health Statistics reported that in 2016, 63,600 persons died of drug overdoses.

Our unbalanced prosperity should trouble us. To ensure continuing resilience, this maldistribution of prosperity needs rectifying. May I suggest that "mine is mine, and I won't share with anybody" is profoundly anti-American? It's about taxation and other mechanisms to protect the wealth of those who already have much more than they need. It runs against our egalitarian instincts for fairness and good citizenship, and we must reject it.

So what to do? The government can change taxes and distribute money to the prosperity-deprived. That doesn't begin to deal with the cultural aspect. It leaves the recipients feeling on the dole and not as hopeful and self-confident members of society. The answer, of course, lies in a massive creation of well-paying jobs. This will demand enhanced education across the board, with special attention to modern skills training for those not choosing college. That will lead large numbers of the poor to join the knowledge-based economy, which otherwise creates disemployment among the undereducated millions.

But why are the poor undereducated? It's the insidious culture that doesn't allow the poorest—Blacks, Whites, and others or Appalachian coal miners—to believe that there is a way out. It's the stagnating mediocrity of the great majority of our schools with their lack of upward aspirations, as described in chapter 5—the tragedy of low expectations. The inspirational book *Hillbilly Elegy*, by J. D. Vance, shows that some can break out. But such individual and exceptional cases unfortunately don't represent the cultural condition of a great resigned majority of the undereducated.

To revitalize and reintegrate the left-behind and the displaced, we must implement without delay a Rebuilding the Workforce Bill, such as I propose in chapter 8. This, of course, is a taxation issue because someone has to pay for major investments in education and training. We must regard it as well-considered, thoughtfully planned prosperity-sharing to the benefit of society, not as socialism. Our culture needs to restore hope and confidence for all Americans. Of course.

The Disunited States of America?

Throughout this book, we trace cultural, social, and economic forces that separate us. Some quite starkly. Red states, blues states, hardly any purple. Why not?

We are divided in our levels of education, which separate us by what we know. We are divided in our views on immigration, the metal that welded America. We are divided by all the cultural fields of battle described in chapter 3: by attitudes to guns and violence, to race and ethnicity; by how we view science and religion; by political ideology; and by concepts of patriotism.

Pretty bleak on the face of it. But perhaps not. Our culture started as White, Anglo-Saxon, Protestant, with a common language and laws from the civilization it brought from England. United as that culture seemed, even then it was divided between North and South, with their different economies and immigration patterns, and between the Atlantic coast, looking out over the ocean to an outside world, and the pioneering West, looking inward. Each had a separate, self-conscious identity that remains with us some 250 years later, expressed as blue and red states.

Yes, but. The current blue/red separations may not be as cut in stone as they may seem to us today. The American Idea is still at work creating new expressions of itself in this ever-dynamic society. A new cultural blend in the multimillions has grown in the country's Southwest, in New Mexico, southern Colorado, Arizona, southern California, and maybe parts of Texas, combining Anglo with Hispanic. They intermarry but remain intensely and uniquely American. Another region, as distinctive as New England, also a long time in the making.

Amazing stability of our Idea over our, by now, long history span. Not so amazing, however, when we consider what kept this culture together. The great majority of Americans held and still holds deeply felt convictions: individual freedom, personal dignity, respect for the law, a common language, belief in fairness. Protestant they all were, except in early Maryland, but immediately numerous Protestant sects emerged, each representing cultural particularities of the meaning of religion. Yet none of these expressions of freedom of thought contradicted their shared common culture.

Over the years came the Germans, the Irish, the Southern and Eastern Europeans, then Latinos and the Asians, and lately Africans. All gradually melted into the national pot after a couple of generations and continue to, persuaded by the power of the Idea. All grafted on the original cultural tree, sharing its beliefs. Tragically, this melting has largely missed American Africans who never asked to be here. Is all that blending still going on today? The emerging Southwest suggests it is. In other regions, like the old Confederacy, perhaps not so much.

Of course, we have little subcultures, especially on academic campuses, who speak badly about evil America. They like to list a catalog of American malfeasance at home and abroad. What an affirmation of our cultural self-assurance and freedom! Let them try it in today's communist China about China.

Let's imagine

Let's look at today's culture as a moving film, projecting its course over the next generation or two.

Experiment in culture #1

American culture, always restless, seeking improvement through change, now calcifies instead in its early twenty-first-century form. We remain divided culturally, politically, educationally, geographically, economically, racially, ethnically, and ideologically, without any of those divisions closing. Many non-Hispanic Whites remain vehemently opposed to diversity, to even legal immigration, and to the "rise" of people of colored skin. Makers resist changes to a hydrocarbon-based economy, while their opponents promote drastic legislation to combat global warming. Those displaced by the economy's drift don't receive retraining and become in effect wards of the state. Social media doesn't become carefully controlled and remains a source of many troubles. Our culture stagnates, deviating from its normal ever-changing evolution that gave primacy to tolerance, forgiveness, openness to the new and the different, and access to opportunity and (mostly) equal justice for all. Will that state of affairs describe our society in, say, 2045?

Experiment in culture #2

The culture continues resilient and remains restless. It seeks and achieves constant change in a quest for better—for better economically, better educationally, better for comforts of life, fairer society, and better justice for all. This produces a turbulent life, with ever-accelerating rhythms stoked by the internet and by technological and scientific prowess. New images appear in the culture's film. New generations, say those born around 2000, think and behave differently than their parents. They become better educated, they marry outside of their ethnic and social tribes, they accept change as normal, not as a departure. They modify the role of social media and place it into a more controlled frame. Differences attenuate as a shared culture makes former divisions less relevant. It's generational change, demographical cohort succession. Not everywhere, not always, but the cumulative effect of these mutations results in the closing of our divisions, the narrowing of our differences. Is that how we will be in 2045?

Which of these two experiments describes the likely course of our culture over the next quarter century? The policies I propose in chapter 8—smart immigration, deep education, science- and knowledge-based economy, enlightened views of the environment, and affirmation of the value of the community—aim to redirect the course of our culture toward experiment #2. What choice will we make?

Chapter 10

So . . . Resilient Still?

————◆————

E pluribus unum?

Does the needle of our compass wobble, or does it still point firmly north?

In the nine preceding chapters, I have chronicled my observations about current America and the state of its resilience. No incontrovertible evidence emerges. Even the four shocks can have opposite effects. For some, they can cause deep despondency, for others a spur to defiant resilience. The same contrasts apply to matters of immigration, education, inventiveness and innovation, economic activities, governance, and the state of our culture.

I have divided this chapter into two main sections: "What works against our resilience" and "Where resilience shines."

The former may represent our future; the latter shows our present. For the former, I say "may," and I want to emphasize the significance of this distinction. All observations I list under the former are manifestations of our discords. They all fall into the realm of beliefs, emotions, and opinions shared at a collective level. But the second section expresses actual behaviors at the individual level.

Where, then, resides our resilience: in changeable collective emotions and beliefs or in culturally ingrained individual actions?

What works against our resilience

Plenty. Basically, all the components I describe in experiment #1 at the end of chapter 9—an America stagnant and divided; that and more.

It's a daunting inventory of shortcomings hampering our resilience. I divide them into two kinds: *snapshots* and *portraits*. Snapshots describe conditions in the early 2020s in the wake of the four shocks from chapter 1. They are hence of recent origin but can affect our future. Portraits describe conditions of long duration and may have begun at the country's very founding. They portray disillusioned citizens who feel loss of hope or reasons for optimism, a decline of faith in democracy, a retreat from shared concerns, skeptical of the assimilative power of the American Idea. In the early 2020s, is what works against our resilience snapshot or portrait? It's some of both.

Polarization

Our polarization stands as the tallest obstacle we need to overcome. While it appears political (blue states/red states, liberals/conservatives), it is actually cultural. Therefore, harder to reduce. The dividing line between blue and red states runs mainly between those engaged in change and those who wish things to remain culturally as they were. These cultural separations appear in our views of education, immigration, science, religion, race, gender, and ethnicity. Many Evangelicals contribute a massive intransigent voice to our divisions, well balanced by the political pressures from the utopian left.

Culture polarizes less obviously too. Let's consider Barack Obama and Donald Trump as cultural polarizers. In Obama's life, his Kenyan father was but a faint episode. His Anglo grandparents brought him up in an Anglo-Saxon traditional ethic. His actions as president fit comfortably in the expected presidential mold, except that society defined him by the color of his skin. For many (e.g., birthers), that polarized. As for Donald Trump, from what we know about his immigrant grandfather and his father, he was from all evidence not brought up in an atmosphere of Anglo-Saxon cultural ethics. As president, he didn't act in the expected mold of his predecessors, all of whom, if not always consciously, acted within the frame of the accepted American culture. Trump's disregard of that culture polarized a majority of Americans. Ironically, millions of Anglo Americans worship Trump as he shreds their cultural norms of honor (by, for instance, dodging the draft or installing lying as his basic political tool).

We had an extended period of polarization for the first
eighty years of the republic, which culminated in the Civil
War. Further events of polarization between the capital-
ist and industrial East and the agricultural West and South
arose in the late nineteenth century. During the twentieth
century, polarization subsided, as in the first two-thirds of
it much social legislation was passed, benefiting a majority,
while the South remained undisturbed. The present polarization is a *snapshot.*

Education

In preceding chapters, I have devoted much attention
to the fact that we are an undereducated nation, not up to
the demands of a knowledge-based twenty-first century.
This condition divides us socially, economically, and politically. Socially, because too many feel left behind; economically, because employment shrinks for the less educated;
and politically, because low-information voters frequently
lack the ability to think critically. Ignorance of and hostility
to science, products of poor secondary or college education,
reduce our supply of scientific minds on which many of our
inventions and our progress depend.

We did better in the past. Appendix 2, with the eighth-
grade final exam from 1895 in Salina, Kansas, shows how
much better prepared the young were for the conditions of
their day. Never has our public education in its overwhelming majority failed as badly as in recent decades. It closes
the doors to opportunity and access to economic equality.
The low unemployment numbers of recent years should not
deceive us. They reflect the buoyance of American business

but not the ongoing *digital* reconfiguring of our economy. That will require more sophisticated workers. The state of our present education is a threatening *snapshot*.

Diversity

Under this label rest additional separations. Some Americans think that all Americans, no matter how "diverse," are equally American. Some think that the "diverse" dilute Anglo-Saxon culture. The very passion of those promoting diversity, racial and ethnic, arouses virulent hostility among millions of their fellow citizens.

Nor are diversity concerns new. Blacks have always borne the brunt of these hostilities, but too many native-born have, since earliest days, viewed persons of non-Anglo stock with wary suspicion. Colonial Pennsylvania didn't welcome Germans or Scots-Irish. The Know-Nothings in the 1850s attributed all troubles to immigrants. In 1924, Congress changed immigration laws to essentially exclude any but northwestern Europeans from immigrating. Resistance to diversity follows a tradition of visceral rejection of the alien. Our present attitudes to diversity are regrettably a *portrait*.

Opposition to immigration

In addition to what I say about diversity, opposition to immigration has deeper consequences. Not only does resistance to immigration by large swaths of natives separate us from each other; it alienates us from the culture that built our national character. In the opening of chapter 4, I describe the foundation of that character as our *immigrant ethic*. We need to revive this ethic because disdain for it saps the moral basis of our society. And we need new immigrants for our economy, our demographic balance, and our spiritual continuity. It's the same *portrait* as in resistance to diversity.

Nonparticipation

An active enemy of resilience is the withdrawal of citizens from participation in society. Tens of millions of Americans today shun civic engagement with the rest of us. It takes several forms.

They don't vote. In November 2020, 63% (159 million) of potential voters voted, the highest in 124 years, which is good for our democracy. Still, it means that 53.5 million Americans decided not to vote—that's four out of ten of us.

Political extremists, some of them terrorists, oppose our current governance by denying the legitimacy of the 2020 election, dramatically so during the assault on the US Capitol on January 6, 2021.

Tragically, many millions declare through their often fatal use of opioids that life in America is not worth living. Milder forms of antisocial feelings expressed themselves in antivaxxers and anti-maskers during covid-19. Aspects of withdrawal from optimism take the form of anxiety and fear around the covid pandemic, some responding in panic. None of this strengthens resilience.

Unhindered participation of all citizens in the governing of our country is the essence of its democracy. The current nonparticipants follow a long tradition. States attempted to secede from the union; over the last hundred-plus years, an average of 40% of Americans didn't vote for president, election after election. That's the normal in our lackadaisical democracy. Nonparticipation is a *portrait*.

Technological disruptions

Computer technology propels us today and influences all aspects of our lives. In earlier chapters, I describe some of the many benefits it brings to us but also its negative effects. Its impact through automation and e-commerce has led to many businesses failing and closing, causing much unemployment and economic damage to individuals. The internet facilitates criminal activities, domestic and foreign, easily concealed. Its algorithms splice us politically—social media as accelerator of partisanship. It divides us economically according to our ability to cope with technological change.

Computer technology leads to invasion of our privacy. It also creates a technological business elite in competition with our government, which it co-opts through political influence. Business has always done that, but never on the scale that computer technology firms can. It is a *snapshot* writ large.

Geographic separations

On America's political map, we see blue and red states. This represents political parties, but our divisions go deeper. Makers of physical things, including agriculture, prevail in some places, brain workers in others. The former in smaller communities, with a prevalence of Anglo culture. The latter in metropolises, breeders of "diversity." Each attracts the like-minded, thereby reinforcing geographic separations.

Throughout their history, Americans have migrated in search of opportunity. Now it appears that they do it more in search of cultural compatibility. So conservative Californians leave their liberal state for more conservative places like Utah or Texas. The Census Bureau reports less migration in search of opportunity. It's a s*napshot.*

Feelings of inequality

Liberal opinion laments our present income distribution inequality. It conflates it with a drastic reduction of opportunity and, for some, the death of the American Dream. The liberal-minded see this situation as unjust and correctable through enlightened legislation. It's more complex. Over recent decades, the globalization of the world economy has motivated businesses and industries to locate across borders. As industries moved, American unions faded. Automation displaced or destroyed white-collar and blue-collar jobs in great numbers. Predictably, comfort in employment has disappeared, and the individual now must make stark personal decisions. It's the result of our restless culture, always seeking to make things more profitable by making them better for the consumer. One result is that those well-educated and willing to assume responsibility for their destiny are well rewarded. Those, however, either educationally ill-prepared or emotionally unmotivated find themselves left behind. This always existed to a degree, but never as strongly as now. It's a *snapshot.*

Government failures

Two of the four shocks chronicled in chapter 1—the Great Recession and covid-19 response—stemmed directly from government failures and thus caused loss of confidence in government among many and in various degrees. Our political dissensions in the 2020s revolve largely around the role of government in our lives: too much of it or not enough; democratic excess, or do we prefer a firmer hand? There are now a very diverse 331 million of us, and our government no longer seems able to provide a supra-partisan, unifying, center-seeking governance. With a smaller, culturally homogeneous population in the past, it could. It's a *snapshot.*

Where resilience shines

The above snapshots and portraits focus on dismal aspects of our resilience. They represent a fixed moment in our time. Meanwhile, as the Mississippi, the course of American destiny just keeps rollin' along. Like a film. it encompasses the full, deep course of American history and features many actors: American enterprising instincts, acceptance of risk and promotion of change, belief in second chances, eagerness to invent and innovate, inmate optimism and self-confidence, dreams of an ever-better future, traits like volunteerism and forgiveness—all components of resilience. Of course, this film includes a couple of the above not-so-resilient portraits.

Spirit

Covid-19 struck; Americans responded immediately, individually and communally. I describe multiple instances of volunteerism in chapter 3, under "Impulse to help strangers." Businesses responded by converting their manufacturing to aid with the pandemic. They made masks and plastic shields. General Motors switched from building certain cars to making ventilators for covid patients. A brewery in Maui, Hawaii, switched from making beer to making disinfectants. Science mobilized for the crisis. Moderna, a small American company in Massachusetts, produced a vaccine in a mere three hundred days using revolutionary scientific principles. It has proved 95% effective. Worth noting, it was also founded by an Armenian immigrant.

No leadership from above caused all this to happen. It arose spontaneously from the constant, resilient American spirit.

Democracy and rule of law

We hear much worry about the state of our democracy and whether it will survive. That is good. We should always worry. Indifference would signal decline in faith. The assault on Congress on January 6, 2021, and new voting rules by Republican state legislatures (targeted restrictions to some, needed control to others) certainly can justify serious concern. But as Mark Twain once remarked, "The news of my death is greatly exaggerated." So is the news of American democracy's ill health. Precisely because we perceived our democracy's potential fragility, a record 66.7% of us came out to vote in November 2020, the highest in 124 years.

Meanwhile, under an unprecedented attack, our institutions and the rule of law have held firm. A president lost his reelection bid by seven million votes in November 2020 but refused to accept the popular verdict, claiming fraud. He and his supporters instituted some sixty lawsuits. Because these were fact-free, the courts rejected all of them, including by judges appointed by that president. Within hours of the mob assault on Congress on January 6, 2021, having been subdued, both chambers of Congress certified the legitimacy of the November 2020 election, confirmed by that president's vice president. Our institutions performed as normal because individuals remained faithful to them.

Business

"The business of America is business," said President Calvin Coolidge ("Silent Cal") in 1925. Indeed, it is—it was then, and it is now. Already in the late eighteenth century, American merchants sailed around the Horn on the China trade. They still trade with China, on a grand scale. In the early 2020s, heedless of snapshots and portraits, they allow their enterprising juices free rein. In covid-wracked 2020, 480 new IPOs were launched, an all-time record, higher by 20% than the previous one in 2000. In that same 2020, 550,000 new business applications were recorded, also a record exceeding by 83% the preceding one in 2019. Venture capitalists still seem giddy. A more dubious record places focus on a serious societal concern. In March 2021, the US Department of Labor announced that the economy had 8.1 million job openings (the previous record was 7.5 million openings in prosperous 2019). This is both good and bad. Good, as an indication of a vibrant economy. Bad, because businesses were unable to fill them all for lack of qualified (or willing?) candidates. (See "Education" above and "Innovation" below.)

Race

I wish I didn't have to touch this festering but, on much current evidence, gradually waning subject that we inherited. Since we deal with resilience, I must. The majority, depending on how one counts, of American Blacks, some 67%, earn middle-level or better (some much better) incomes. There are those who don't want to hear such news, but when I arrived in the United States some sixty years ago, such news was scarcely imaginable. Now we have celebrated Black authors, musicians, distinguished generals, engineers, and scientists. Millions of Blacks have graduated from college. Time to celebrate? Not yet. Racist animus still lurks in darker corners of our society, and large segments of the Black population are still mired in poverty and ignorance. But the majority are making the transition into society's middle stream. They may not have heard that America is in decline. That is a case to rejoice.

Inventiveness and innovation

In October 2020, Jennifer Doudna, professor of biochemistry at the University of California, Berkeley, received the Nobel Prize for Chemistry. It recognized her co-discovery of mechanisms of gene sequencing (genetic engineering). This discovery holds momentous potential for medicine and for society. Doudna's achievement is part of a much larger set of research in the field of gene modification by American scientists. Many have patented their discoveries and founded innovative companies, bringing the benefits of basic research science to the public in practical form. Vitality of a knowledge society.

We also innovate when ponderous government at all levels has failed to respond to our education, training, and retraining needs. Innovators have stepped in, as I describe in chapter 6 under "Worker displacement." Businesses like IBM and private entrepreneurs have created new educational programs that provide job preparedness for a science- and technology-led economy.

NASA (that, too, is all of us) is building the gigantic James Webb Space Telescope. It will be the largest, most powerful, and most complex space telescope ever built. When launched into space, it will forever alter our understanding of the universe. We build it because Americans think exuberantly and think into the future, an attitude of resilience.

The young

Attention to resilience is about the future and hence about our young. Someday they'll run the country; meanwhile they think differently. In conversations with them and in surveys about them, certain themes surface. They are largely indifferent to the political separations that agitate their elders. Our present divisive politics don't seem to touch them. That includes frictions about race, ethnicity, and diversity. In fact, many young intermarry across those lines—in 2015, 16% of marriages.[6] That year, such unions produced 14% of babies born.[7] The young worry, if at all, about saving the planet, not about the various snapshots I list above. If coming together in a commonly shared culture energizes resilience, then the young contribute their part. Some headlines from the Pew Research Center's surveys:

- "Younger Americans are better than older Americans at telling factual news statements from opinion."

- "Younger adults differ from older in their perceptions of covid-19 and of George Floyd protests."

- "Younger people are less religious than older ones, especially in the US, but also in most of Europe."

- "A wider partisan and ideological gap between younger and older generations."

- "Younger Americans (18–29) more likely to read the news; older to watch."

- "Younger Americans (under 30) engage with public libraries."

- "Younger voters return to the voting booth (unlike in many decades)."

But

- "Younger people less knowledgeable." (If you
  doubt, see appendix 2.)

- "Younger Americans more likely than older
  to say that other countries better than US."

Of course, some passionately support current ideologically fashionable bubbles, as the young always have.

Signals from the culture

Our resilience resides in our culture. That culture sends
us signals, some foreboding like the snapshots and portraits
above. Other signals suggest promising outcomes. Are we
looking optimistically into the future, or do we feel pessi-
mistically stuck in the past? Do we exhibit symptoms of evolution and adaptability? Can-do or no-can-do? What about
the American Dream? Let's examine culture's signals that
bespeak resilience. Perhaps the degrees of our engagements
and how we adapt and evolve tell us how sturdy our resilience remains.

Engaging socially

Covid-19 tested Americans' civic instincts and didn't
find them wanting. They mobilized, as I describe in chapter
3 under "An impulse to help strangers." They bring support,
they give money, they risk their lives as nurses volunteer their
services in distant cities. The national character surfaced
spontaneously. At an individual level often, probably over-
riding politics.

Engaging in education and training

Reformist educators, concerned parents, philanthropic citizens (as well as foundations and businesses) have addressed our critical educational needs in recent decades and continue to produce needed changes and educational innovations, which I report in chapters 5, under "The good," and 6, under "Worker displacement."

Engaging economically

American investors and venture capitalists appear unfazed by the covid-19 economy—in fact, stimulated by its fallout. Where some spirits may fall, the American opportunity-perceiving instincts rise. See the amazingly exuberant numbers of startups and new business applications in 2020 in chapter 7 under "Entrepreneurial instincts and investor spirits." *The Economist* informed us on September 18, 2021, that in the first six months of that year 2.8 million new firms were born in the US. Reality may yet disappoint, but business resilience is up.

Engaging when aged and when young too

Many millions of our seniors work, teach, volunteer, and vote, the last more than any other age group. They continue to energize our society and show commitment to it, as we see in chapter 9 under "The aging of our population."(I even know a ninety-year-old who is writing a book.) The young turn their attention to the future, as is normal, and mostly ignore the political bickering of their elders. And they vote. Historically, they have voted very little, rarely exceeding 40% of their age group. But 53% did in November 2020, a higher

commitment to the country's political processes by historical standards. While voting perhaps does not express resilience, when the young do it in increased numbers, it sends an
encouraging social message.

Adapting and evolving

The culture also sends a message about the power of the
American Idea and its adaptability and vitality. As we see in
chapter 9 (under "The Disunited States of America?"), the
Southwest has formed another manifestation of American
identity. The region comprising southern California, Arizona,
New Mexico, southern Colorado, and western Texas, sunny
lands bordering on Mexico, has evolved, over the past 150
years, a distinct culture. Its denizens intermarry between
the numerous Hispanics with non-Hispanics, producing a
unique blend of Americans. After one generation, all speak
English. The emerging culture often produces stable families.
Although Amerindians remain a society apart.

Steady

As the four shocks begin to recede, society emerges
severely divided. Individuals, however, continue on their
steady American march, regardless of their political views.
The media, formal and social, show a nation anxious to
resume normal life—working, schooling, investing, getting
married, caring about their young—to recover lost time.
They shop online, vote in large numbers, congregate on
Zoom when not doing so in person, and engage in distance
learning. And attend baseball games. That desire to recover
normality is resilience too.

Resilient, then, or not?

So, reader, decide for yourself. Do the snapshots and portraits, seemingly rooted in our current culture, depict our
reality and point to our future?

In a quest for a shared civic center where our resilience
dwells, we meet our culture's hard-to-overcome obstacles:
ethno-racial animus, political dissensions, socioeconomic
disparities, violence (both criminal and political), and patriotic ideas about flag and anthem. Are these obstacles in our
destiny? Is our polarization terminal? Are gun control and
abortion unsurmountable barriers? Are extreme political
passions from right and left and the rest of us in a fragile
middle our destiny?

Or do you find more persuasive the elements I describe
above under "Where resilience shines?" Actions of individuals: educators, entrepreneurs, investors, volunteers, voters,
philanthropists, inventors and innovators, and average
Americans. Decide whether the rolling film of the can-do,
optimistic national character still represents an uninterrupted, resilient continuity.

What must we do?

To those who ask that question, my suggestion is to keep
their faith in the extraordinarily successful social experiment that is the United States of America. It is undergoing its
periodic convulsions and needs individual support. Losing
faith in it will not help resilience. On a collective label,
work on implementing the policy and legislation proposals
I present in chapter 8.

For my part, I conclude with:

Perseverance and *Ingenuity*

Though they hint at American character traits, in this case, these words don't define abstract ideas. They are the names of two American spacecrafts exploring the planet Mars. Congress, otherwise partisan, has united in funding this mission in the multibillions. Why? National prestige? National sense of mission? Does such adventurous pursuit of basic scientific knowledge describe a people in decline, crouched defensively, peering anxiously into the future? Fearing China? Unable to muster resilience? A great nation doesn't just try to survive. It holds a loftier view of its destiny.

Acknowledgments

———— ◆ ————

This book has greatly benefited from the careful reading and thoughtful critique of an exceptional group of friends. They have read all or portions of my manuscript and offered incisive insights across the American political spectrum. I also had extensive conversations with several of them. They are:

Craig Barth
Jennie Burger
Skip Bushee
Bea Gormley
Bob Gormley
Mary Lewis Grow
Carolyn Crockett Lewis
John Lewis
Jerry Rudisin
Michael Victor

Mere words cannot fully express the depth of my appreciation. Of course, any inadequacies are entirely my own. I must acknowledge also some sixty years of intense and interested observation of the American people. They inspire this book.

Appendix 1

Frequency of Economic Crises

Note the extreme frequency of economic crises, particularly in the early years, when the economy was unregulated. As more laws were enacted to regulate the economy, the recessions became less frequent but more severe. From 1920 on, I don't record the frequent small recessionary tremors that lasted a few months and had no notable consequences.[1]

Type	Years lasted	Year stated	Year ended
Panic—uncertainty of a new country	4	1785	1789
Panic—counterfeiting of copper coins	4	1789	1793
Panic—investment bubble	1	1796	1797
Recession—European wars	2	1802	1804

Type	Years lasted	Year stated	Year ended
Depression—conflicts w/ Britain	1	1807	1807
Recession—War of 1812	1	1812	1812
Depression—economic factors, inflation	6	1815	1821
Recession—commodity prices	2	1822	1823
Recession—stock market, spec. bubble	2	1825	1826
Recession—trade w/ Britain	2	1828	1829
Recession—credit restrictions	2	1833	1834
Recession—loss of confidence, bank runs	2	1836	1838
Recession—monetary downturn	4	1840	1843
Recession—economic turbulence	2	1847	1848
Recession—rising interest rates	1	1853	1854
Panic—trade w/ Europe	1	1857	1857
Recession (brief)	1	1860	1861
Recession—after-war deflation	2	1865	1867
Recession—market speculations	1	1869	1870
Depression—fallout from bank failure	6	1873	1879
Recession—bank failure and panic	3	1882	1885
Recession—economic turbulence	2	1887	1888

Type	Years lasted	Year stated	Year ended
Recession—minor	1	1890	1891
Panic—savings/gold, bank failures	4	1893	1897
Recession—stock market crash	2	1902	1904
Panic—financial shenanigans	1	1907	1907
Panic—Sherman Antitrust Act	2	1910	1911
Recession—economy in decline	2	1913	1914
Recession—postwar effects	1	1918	1919
Depression—postwar effects	1.5	1920	1921
Recession—mild	1	1923	1824
Recession—minor	1	1928	1927
Great Depression—stock market	9	1929	1938
Recession—federal policy on interests	1	1948	1949
Recession—Korean War	1	1953	1954
Recession—federal policy	1	1957	1958
Recession—federal policy	1	1950	1961
Recession—Vietnam War	1	1969	1970
Recession—Arab oil embargo	1.5	1973	1975
Recession—government policies	1	1981	1982
Recession—dot-com bubble	1	2000	2001
Recession—subprime mortgages	1.5	2007	2009
Recession—covid-19		2020	

Appendix 2

The Eighth-Grade Final Exam from 1895 in Salina, Kansas

Taken from the original document on file at the Smoky [sic] Valley Genealogical Society and Library in Salina and reprinted by the *Salina Journal*.

Grammar (Time, one hour):

1. Give nine rules for the use of capital letters.
2. Name the parts of speech and define those that have no modifications.
3. Define verse, stanza and paragraph.
4. What are the principal parts of a verb? Give principal parts of "lie," "play," and "run."
5. Define case; illustrate each case.
6. What is punctuation? Give rules for principal marks of punctuation.

7–10. Write a composition of about 150 words and show therein that you understand the practical use of the rules of grammar.

Arithmetic (Time, 1 hour 15 minutes)

1. Name and define the Fundamental Rules of Arithmetic.
2. A wagon box is 2 ft. deep, 10 feet long, and 3 ft. wide. How many bushels of wheat will it hold?
3. If a load of wheat weighs 3,942 lbs, what is it worth at 50 cts/bushel, deducting 1,050 lbs for tare?
4. District No 33 has a valuation of $35,000. What is the necessary levy to carry on a school seven months at $50 per month, and have $104 for incidentals?
5. Find the cost of 6,720 lbs coal at $6.00 per ton.
6. Find the interest of $512.60 for 8 months and 18 days at 7 percent per annum.
7. What is the cost of 40 boards 12 inches wide and 16 ft long at $20 per meter?
8. Find bank discount on $300 for 90 days (no grace) at 10 percent.
9. What is the cost of a square farm at $15 per acre, the distance of which is 640 rods?
10. Write a bank check, a promissory note, and a receipt.

US History (Time, 45 minutes)

1. Give the epochs into which US history is divided.
2. Give an account of the discovery of America by Columbus.
3. Relate the causes and results of the Revolutionary War.
4. Show the territorial growth of the United States.
5. Tell what you can of the history of Kansas.
6. Describe three of the most prominent battles of the Rebellion.

7. Who were the following: Morse, Whitney, Fulton, Bell, Lincoln, Penn, and Howe?

8. Name events connected with the following dates: 1607, 1620, 1800, 1849, 1865.

Orthography (Time, one hour)

[Author's note: Do we even know what this is?]

1. What is meant by the following: alphabet, phonetic, orthography, etymology, syllabication?

2. What are elementary sounds? How classified?

3. What are the following, and give examples of each: trigraph, subvocals, diphthong, cognate letters, linguals?

4. Give four substitutes for caret "u."

5. Give two rules for spelling words with final "e." Name two exceptions under each rule.

6. Give two uses of silent letters in spelling. Illustrate each.

7. Define the following prefixes and use in connection with a word: bi, dis, pre, semi, post, non, inter, mono, sup.

8. Mark diacritically and divide into syllables the following, and name the sign that indicates the sound: card, ball, mercy, sir, odd, cell, rise, blood, fare, last.

9. Use the following correctly in sentences: cite, site, sight, fane, fain, feign, vane, vain, vein, raze, raise, rays.

10. Write 10 words frequently mispronounced and indicate pronunciation by use of diacritical marks and by syllabication.

Geography (Time, one hour)

1. What is climate? Upon what does climate depend?
2. How do you account for the extremes of climate in Kansas?
3. Of what use are rivers? Of what use is the ocean?
4. Describe the mountains of North America.
5. Name and describe the following: Monrovia, Odessa, Denver, Manitoba, Hecla, Yukon, St. Helena, Juan Fernandez, Aspinwall and Orinoco.
6. Name and locate the principal trade centers of the US. Name all the republics of Europe and give the capital of each.
8. Why is the Atlantic Coast colder than the Pacific in the same latitude?
9. Describe the process by which the water of the ocean returns to the sources of rivers.
10. Describe the movements of the earth. Give the inclination of the earth.

Appendix 3

Second Amendment and Other Archaic Notions

After one mass shooting, New Zealand banned assault weapons.

After one mass shooting, Canada banned assault weapons.

But after 107 mass shootings by mid-2021 alone,[1] the United States has still not banned assault weapons . . . because the Second Amendment reigns.

Indeed, almost every day, the media reports a mass shooting somewhere in the country. Ho-hum. The FBI reports (June 2021) that mass shootings in the United States between 2000 and 2018 produced 2,437 casualties in 277 incidents. It happened in schools, churches, businesses, government, and post offices. The years 2017 and 2018 were the worst, with thirty and twenty-seven major incidents, respectively. It's growing, but ho-hum.

Consider:

Year	Killed	Wounded
2018	80	66
2017	112	531
2016	71	83
2015	46	43
2014	17	28
2013	31	13
2012	67	68
2011	18	21
2010	8	2
2009	38	37
2008	16	24

This table lists only "major shooting events."

A CNN headline (June 12, 2021): "Violence in Texas, Georgia and Illinois brings the number of mass shootings in the U.S. to 267 so far this year."[2] Ho-hum. What's a few lives if we can preserve the sacredness of the Second Amendment?

The Second Amendment

This amendment to the US Constitution divides us sharply at a time when we need to erase divisions. Its supporters and its opponents see no common ground on this archaic creation of our governance. The Second was established to create militias—not to combat a foreign enemy but to suppress slave uprising primarily in the South.[3] The presumed need for militias, not that they ever saw action, vanished with the Civil War. So how to explain the survival of the Second Amendment?

Like apple pie, violence, and firearms

On June 2, 2021, in Volusia County, Florida, a twelve-year-old boy and a fourteen-year-old girl opened fire on sheriff's deputies with stolen guns, including an AK-47. Ho-hum.

America, let's face it, is a violent society. Love of guns has been with us longer than the proverbial apple pie. Firearm violence grew from our very beginning, in the seventeenth century. Ever since, we've murdered each other, but Amerindians particularly, abundantly and systematically. In California, 49ers would hunt Amerindians for Sunday recreation. The settling of the frontier from colonial days occurred violently more often than not. Then Manifest Destiny justified force for many, and we attacked Mexico. The history of the nineteenth-century West was written by Colts, Winchesters, and Remingtons and not by ploughs and schoolmarms alone.

Firearms kill Americans—39,740 in 2018.[4] These deaths stem from various causes: individual or gang-related murders, mass shooting, accidents, and suicides. The numbers keep rising. While in 2012, 2013, and 2014, such deaths were in the thirty-three-thousand-plus range, by 2017, they had increased to 39,773. Two-thirds of them are generally attributed to suicides.[5]

Most menacing to the general public are mass shootings, whose mounting frequency and growing tolls have frighteningly proliferated in the most recent decade. These mass murders are committed for ideological as well as psychopathological reasons and spare no one. Often, they target children in schools.

If one hundredth of the above numbers was perpetrated by, say, an Islamic group, we would term it terrorism. In fact, we have cossetted domestic terrorism, abetted by politics of war-caliber firearm proliferation. Terrorism born from ideology and from psychopathology.

American opinion splits between those who assign the responsibility for this state of affairs to an uncontrolled access to guns and those who defend Second Amendment rights uncompromisingly. Those concerned with the right to bear arms recommend "thoughts and prayers." They reserve their ire for advocates of gun control. This results in a rigid cleavage, and rigidity is the enemy of resilience.

Endnotes

Chapter 1

1 The *Encyclopedia Britannica* offers a detailed account of the Tea Party. See https://www.britannica.com/topic/Tea-Party-movement.

2 Gretchen Morgenson and Joshua Rosner, *Reckless Endangerment: How Outsized Ambition, Greed, and Corruption Led to Economic Armageddon* (Time Books, Henry Holt and Co., New York, 2017).

3 Morgenson, *Reckless Endangerment*.

4 Johan Norberg, *Open: The Story of Human Progress* (Atlantic Books, London, 2020). See in particular chapter 8, in which Norberg discusses the rise of White racism in economically rough times.

5 Isabel Wilkerson, *Caste: The Origins of Our Discontents* (Random House, New York, 2020). This offers the Black perspective on the racial climate during these events.

6 John Steinbeck's classic *The Grapes of Wrath* powerfully depicts the meeting of the two Americas in California during the Depression.

7 *The Economist*, "Dollar Swap Lines" (June 20, 2020). This article reports on how quickly and effectively the Federal Reserve reassured the world economy by stabilizing the dollar in the middle of the covid crisis.

8 *New York Times*, "How Americans feel about the country right now" (June 27, 2020). "Anxious," and "hopeful" capture their national mood in mid-pandemic. Even then resilience lived.

Chapter 2

1 Upton Sinclair, *The Jungle* (1906). Available from Amazon in hardback and paperback. A novel that had a strong social and regulatory repercussion.

2 John Steinbeck, *The Grapes of Wrath*. See chapter 1 above.

3 Studs Terkel, *Hard Times*. A powerful tribute to the American spirit, available from Amazon in paper and Kindle format.

4 James McGovern, *A Time for Hope: Americans in the Great Depression*. Unfortunately pretty much out of print.

5 No history of the United States from John Kennedy's assassination and the late 1970s had been published at the time of this writing. History must mark those years as the turning point when modern America had its tumultuous birth.

6 Sean Bryant, "How Many States Fail and Why," Investopedia (November 20, 2020). The article reports, "Research concludes 21.5% of startups fail in the first year, 30% in the second year, 50% in the fifth year, and 70% in their 10th year."

7 *Forbes*'s lists of the four hundred richest Americans in

1996 and 2021 shed some light. Some 70% of the names recur, but the richest in 1996 hold lesser positions in 2021. Significantly, of the top ten names in 1996, only three recur in 2021: Gates, Buffett, and Ellison; the other seven have receded, replaced by entirely new names: Bezos, Zuckerberg, Balmer, Musk, Page, and Brin. There remain many "one-percenters" with inherited money, but their positions have faded from 1996 to 2021, and 30% of names from 1996 have vanished from the 2021 list.

8 *Black Demographics*, August 12, 2020.

9 *Black Demographics.*

10 *Black Demographics.*

11 First number from the *Washington Post* (August 28,2013), the second from the US Census Bureau.

12 In *The Long Game* (Oxford University Press, 2021), Rush Doshi speculates that if China prevails over the coming decades, as it intends to, the United States will become reduced to a "deindustrialized, English-speaking version of a Latin American republic, specializing in commodities, real estate, tourism and perhaps transnational tax evasion."

Chapter 3

1 Business Insider, "2020 saw more gun deaths in the US than any year in over two decades, showing even a pandemic couldn't stop the violence" (March 23, 2021).

2 The Economist, "Southern Baptists: A house divided.

America's largest Protestant denomination holds off an insurgency" (June 19, 2021).

3   A typical representative of that genre is Noam Chomsky, *Requiem for the American Dream: The 10 Principles of Concentration of Wealth & Power* (2016), on Kindle only from Amazon.

4   Pew Research Center, "Most Think the 'American Dream' is within reach for them" (October 31, 2017).

5   Alexis de Tocqueville, *Democracy in America*. Nearly two centuries after its publication in the early 1830s, it remains the sharpest collection of observations about the American character and American culture. It is still valid for me today.

6   PBS Frontline, "Camp Fire by the Numbers" (October 29, 2019).

7   "Camp Fire by the Numbers."

8   https://doi.org/share.america.gov.

9   Robert Putnam, *Bowling Alone: The Collapse and Revival of the American Community* (Simon & Schuster, New York, 2000).

10 Pew Research Center, telephone interviews in 2018 and 2020.

Chapter 4

1   Pew Research Center, "How many Americans know since 2019."

2   Foundation for Economic Education, "By the Numbers: Do Immigrants Cause Crime?" (July 13, 2015).

3   See also Conference Board "Labor Shortages Are Making a Comeback" (May 25, 2021).

4   Business Roundtable, "The Skills Gap Explained." https://www.businessroundtable.org/policy.

5   "The Skills Gap Explained."

6   Smithsonian Science Education, "The TEM imperative." Other sources project 2.4 million unfilled STEM positions in the United States in 2018.

7   Usha Lee McFarling, "Nursing Ranks Are Filled with Filipino Americans," STAT (March 28, 2020). https://www.statnews.com/staff/usha-mcfarling.

8   CNBC, "US Birth and Fertility Rates Fell to Another Record Low, CDC Says" (May 5, 2021).

9   Population Reference Bureau, "PRB 2010 World Population Data Sheet: 'Fewer and Fewer Workers to Support Aging Population'" (July 28, 2010).

10 "PRB 2010 World Population Data Sheet."

11 Steven A. Camarota and Karen Zeigler, "Fertility Rates among Immigrants and Native-born Americans," Center for Immigration Studies (February 16, 2021).

12 Center for Immigration Studies, "63% of Non-Citizen Households Access Welfare Programs" (November 20, 2018).

13 Isabel Wilkerson, *The Warmth of Other Suns: The Epic Story of America's Great Migration* (Random House, New York, 2002).

14 "Canada Enticing Skilled Workers," *San Francisco Chronicle* (August 10, 2020).

15 American Immigration Council Security, "The U.S. Economy Still Needs Highly Skilled Foreign Workers" (March 30, 2011).

16 Department of Homeland Security Yearbook of

Immigrations Statistics, "Table 6: Persons Obtaining Lawful Permanent Residence . . . Years 2017, 2018, 2019."

17   Center for Immigration Studies, "Welfare Use by Immigrant and Native Households" (September 10, 2015).

Chapter 5

1   Smithsonian Magazine, "One in Four Americans Haven't Read a Book Last Year" (September 2, 2016).

2   Harvard University, Center on the Developing Child, "In Brief: the Science of Early Childhood Development" and Wisconsin Council on Children and Family, "Brain Development and Early Learning" 1 (winter 2007).

3   Teresa McIntire, "Study on Vocabulary Development," famailies.com, 2007.

4   Karen Weintraub, "The Adult Brain Does Grow New Neurons After All, Study Says," *Scientific America* (March 25, 2019).

5   An updated version of these data appears in National ACT, *The Condition of College and Career Readiness 2019*.

6   Data for 2019 appear in NAEP, *Report Cards for Science, Reading and Mathematics.*

7   National Center for Education Statistics (NCES), see *Fast Facts—Expenditures*. From the IES NCES report of May 2020: "In 2016, the United States spent $13,600 per full-time-equivalent (FTE) student on elementary and secondary education, which was 39 percent higher than the average of Organization for Economic Cooperation and Development (OECD) member countries of $9,800 (in constant 2018 U.S. dollars). At the postsecondary

level, the United States spent $31,600 per FTE student, which was 95 percent higher than the average of OECD countries ($16,200)."

8   Newsweek, "AP Programs Participation and Performance 2018, Summary Reports."

9   Newsweek, "AP Programs Participation."

10 College Board, Class of 2018/AP Results: Capstone Expansion. https://reports.collegeboard.org/archive/2018/ap

11 Theodore Sizer, *Horace's Compromise: The Dilemma of the American High School* (Houghton-Mifflin, Boston, 1984). Highly recommended to understand the state of our secondary education.

Chapter 6

1   "The History of the Assembly Line and Interchangeable Parts." www.partsgeek.com/mmparts/history_of_the_assembly_line.html

2   US Patent Office, "US Patent Applications, Calendar Year 1790 to the Present."

3   Pew Research Center, "How many Americans know since 2019."

4   David Ewing Duncan, "216 Million Americans Citizens Are Scientifically Ignorant (Part I)," *MIT Technology Review* (February 21, 2007).

5   National Science Foundation data. (ncses.nsf.gov/pubs/nsf20301/technical-notes) and American Mathematical Society, "The Mathematical and Statistical Sciences Annual Survey."

6   Information Technology & Innovation Foundation,

"The Demographics of Innovation in the United States," (February 24, 2016).

7   Forbes, "Immigrants, Nobel Prizes and the America Dream" (October 14, 2020).

8   B. Herold, "Technology in Education: An Overview," *Education Week* (February 4, 2016). http://www.edweek. org/ew/issues/technology-in-education

9   Herold, "Technology in Education."

Chapter 7

1   Monica Anderson and Madhumitha Kumar, "Digital Divide Persists," Pew Research Center, FactTank (May 7, 2019).

2   William H. Davidow and M. Malone, *The Autonomous Revolution* (Berrett-Koehler Publishers, 2020). An excellent, in-depth discussion of the effects of automation on society.

3   Davidow and Malone, *The Autonomous Revolution.* A very good discussion of the multiplier effect on pp. 102–103, 194.

4   Robotic Industries Association, "Why Robotic Automation Is the Future of Manufacturing" (June 25, 2019).

5   Fortune, "Gig Economy Statistics: The New Normal in the Workplace" (May 19, 2020). Very good discussion of the topic.

6   MBO Partners, *The State of Independence in America 2018: The New Normal.* Excellent in-depth discussion of gig work, present and projected.

7   Statista, "Health industry statistics" (June 8, 2020).

8   CDC Library, "Covid-19 Science Update" (December 15, 2020).

9   Steven E. Koonin, *Unsettled: What Climate Science Tells Us, What It Doesn't, and Why It Matters* (BenBella Books, Dallas, 2020). An in-depth, data-based discussion of climate modeling.

10 National Institute on Drug Abuse, Overdose Death Rates. https://www.drugabuse.gov/drug-topics/trends-statistics/overdose-death-rates.

Chapter 8

1   The Economist, "How TSMC has mastered the geopolitics of chipmaking" (April 9, 2021).

2   USA Facts, "4.4 million American households with children don't have consistent access to computers for online learning during the pandemic" (September 28, 2020).

3   US Small Business Administration, Release No. 19–1 Adv, "Small Business Generates 44 Percent of U.S. Economic Activity" (June 20, 2019).

4   Steven E. Koonin, *Unsettled: What Climate Science Tells Us, What It Doesn't, and Why It Matters* (BenBella Books, Dallas, 2020). A careful, data-based, dispassionate examination of climate change.

5   Daveed Gartenstein-Ross, "Terrorists Are Going to Use Artificial Intelligence," *Defense One* (June 3, 2018). A useful discussion of the internet's potential for terrorism and subversion.

Chapter 9

1   Two books detail the subversive activities of the Russian government on the internet. They are *Active Measures, the History of Disinformation and Political Warfare*, by Thomas Rid (2020), and *The Folly and the Glory: America, Russia and Political warfare, 1945–2020*, by Tim Weiner (2020).

2   The majority/minority discussion relies on combined data from the US Census Bureau, the American Community Survey, and the Current Population Survey.

3   Brookings, "Why Census Is Right to Ask for Racial and Ethnic Data" (March 16, 2007). This article expresses the views of liberal pressure groups influencing the classifications of the Census Bureau.

4   Population Reference Bureau's *Population Bulletin*, June 2019, "Aging in the United States," examines recent trends and disparities among adults ages sixty-five and older and how baby boomers born between 1946 and 1964 are reshaping America's older population.

5   Joel Kotkin, "Economic Civil War: Inside the Bitter Battle over America's New Geography," *American Mind* (February 23, 2021).

6   NPR, "Steep Rise in Interracial Marriages among Newlyweds 50 Years after They Became Legal" (May 18, 2017).

7   Kimberly Yan, "Number of Multiethnic and Multiracial Babies Triples in 35 Years," *HuffPost* (June 16, 2017).

Appendix 1

1 Angela Underwood, "Every recession in country's history and how the country responded," *Stacker* (August 29, 2020).

Appendix 3

1 Chris Wilson, "Why Are There So Many Conflicting Numbers of Mass Shootings?" *TIME Magazine* (April 17, 2021).

2 The numbers of mass shootings differ by source, depending on how each defines mass shootings. I prefer FBI data from US Department of Justice annual reports.

3 Carl Anderson, *The Second, Race and Guns in a Fatally Unequal America*, on Kindle from Amazon. A documented chronicle of the reasons for the creation of the Second Amendment.

4 Daniel Nass, "Gun Deaths Again Neared 40,000 in 2018, CDC Data Shows," *The Trace* (February 12, 2020).

5 Nass, "Gun Deaths."

Index

Note: Page numbers followed by *t* refer to tables.